Robin Ward is a writer, graphic designer and architecture critic, born and raised in Glasgow. He took a gap year to the Canadian north, as a fur-trading clerk for the Hudson's Bay Company, and travelled across Canada before returning to Scotland to study at Glasgow School of Art. His interest in architecture was inspired by a high school trip to Basil Spence's Coventry Cathedral, study at the Mackintosh Building at the GSA and a post-graduate scholarship to Italy. He wrote and illustrated a column for the *Herald* (Glasgow), worked in London as a designer with the BBC and relocated to Vancouver in 1988. He has travelled widely in Canada, Europe and South-east Asia (he married into a Thai family). For 10 years, he was the architecture critic at *The Vancouver Sun*. He has received awards for design, illustration and journalism, including a Heritage Canada Achievement Award and a prize in *The Architectural Review* Centenary Drawing Competition. He is based in Edinburgh.

Other books by this author:
Exploring Glasgow: The Architectural Guide 2017
Exploring Bangkok: An Architectural and Historical Guidebook 2014
Exploring Vancouver: The Architectural Guide (as co-writer) 1993; 2012
Echoes of Empire: Victoria and Its Remarkable Buildings 1996
Robin Ward's Heritage West Coast 1993
Some City Glasgow 1982; 1988

Office pods for Members of the Scottish Parliament mimic the crowstep gables in the Old Town.

Exploring
Edinburgh

Six Tours of the City and its Architecture

Robin Ward

Luath Press Limited
EDINBURGH
www.luath.co.uk

First published in 2021

ISBN 978-1-913025-57-1

British Library Cataloguing-in-Publication Data: a catalogue record for this book is available from the British Library.

The paper used in this book is recyclable. It is made from low chlorine pulps produced in a low energy, low emission manner from renewable forests.

Printed and bound by Bell & Bain Ltd, Glasgow.

Designed and typeset in Myriad Pro by Robin Ward.

Robin Ward's right to be identified as the author of this work has been asserted by him in accordance with the Copyright, Designs and Patents Act 1988. All rights reserved. No part of this publication may be reproduced, stored or transmitted in any form without the express written permission of the publisher.

Text, photographs (except as indicated below) and maps copyright © Robin Ward 2020.

The following copyright © images are reproduced courtesy of the Scottish Parliamentary Corporate Body, *entry 3 (aerial photograph)*; Page\Park Architects, photographer Andrew Lee *128, 265 (Rosslyn Chapel interior)*; Elder & Cannon Architects *256 (school)*; Porta Ward *101 (soldier), 102, 110, 111 (lane), 112, 116, 117 (statue), 132, 134, 269.*

MIX
Paper from
responsible sources
FSC
www.fsc.org   FSC® C007785

Contents

The West Front, St Giles' High Kirk decorated with gargoyles and statues of Scottish monarchs and clergymen. Above the door is St Giles, Edinburgh's patron saint, with the deer he saved from hunters.

Introduction

Around 1830, St Giles' High Kirk, Edinburgh's 'mother church', was given a Gothic Revival facelift. Only the 15th-century crown steeple was untouched. In 1884, the west front was rebuilt in medieval style. The kirk's authentic medieval appearance, weathered over centuries, was wiped away.

Like St Giles', much of the Old Town is a Victorian fantasy, with buildings designed in the romantic Scots Baronial style. The main street is the Royal Mile – Castlehill, the Lawnmarket, High Street and the Canongate – arrow-straight from Edinburgh Castle to the Stuart dynasty's palace in Holyrood Park. From 1860 to 1900, two-thirds of the Old Town's medieval buildings were torn down for slum clearance and civic improvement; only 78 pre-1750 survive. Of 200 or so closes – the shadowy alleys and entrances to tenements – around 80 remain. They branch off perpendicular to the Royal Mile, some precipitous. Many are named after their builders or residents: for example, Advocates', Brodie's, Lady Stair's, or for their commercial links – Fishmarket, Fleshmarket, Sugarhouse. Their medieval pattern is unchanged. Some are said to be haunted.

Old Edinburgh was nicknamed 'Auld Reekie', a reference to the stink before modern sanitation was introduced, and smoke from coal fires that once lingered like fog above the tenements. Robert Louis Stevenson described them, in *Edinburgh, Picturesque Notes*, as 'smoky beehives, ten stories high'. They were a response to topography: the Old Town tumbles down a steep-sided volcanic ridge on which the only way to accommodate the growing population was to build high.

By the mid 18th century, this dense, overcrowded environment was unsustainable. Lord Provost George Drummond visualised a new town and promoted a design competition for it. The New Town Plan of 1767 showed a rational grid of spacious streets, subsequently lined with

Georgian architecture – an alternative, for those who could afford it, to the Old Town where rich and poor scurried around amidst opulence and squalor.

The New Town Plan was a symbol of the Age of Enlightenment, the revival of classical culture in which Scotland played a significant role. More than any other European city, Edinburgh expressed the Enlightenment in architecture. The design of the National Monument (to the fallen of the Napoleonic Wars) on Calton Hill was copied from the Parthenon; the Royal Scottish Academy and the National Gallery on The Mound are also Greek Revival in style. The city acquired a new nickname – the 'Athens of the North'.

The Old and New Towns are separated by a glacial valley drained of its Nor (North) Loch and landscaped in the 19th century to create Princes Street Gardens, one of the world's great urban parks. Railway tracks to Waverley Station were laid in the 1840s, hidden from view in a cutting below Castle Rock. The station was named after the *Waverley* novels of Walter Scott. His monument, a fantastic Gothic pinnacle, punctuates the park. This terrific townscape – Castle Rock, the Old Town, Calton Hill, the New Town and Princes Street Gardens – was declared in 1995 a UNESCO World Heritage Site.

Edinburgh's narrative of enlightenment and cultural heritage ignores many ghosts. Those at Sugarhouse Close are from the slave trade – sugar produced by African slaves on colonial plantations in the West Indies was processed at a refinery in the close. Many of the plantations were owned by Scottish merchants. Glasgow's complicity in transatlantic slavery is acknowledged. Edinburgh has recently been forced to face up to its involvement.

Slavey in English (later British) colonies gained royal patronage in the 1660s when Charles II granted a charter to (and invested in) what became the Royal African Company. The trade continued until 1807 when the Abolition of the Slave Trade Act was passed. Ownership of slaves was not abolished until 1833, and then only because the British government agreed to compensate not the slaves but their owners. The payout was £20 million (40 percent of the Treasury's annual budget at the time). Around half of the claimants in Edinburgh gave addresses in the New Town. Profits from plantations and participation in British imperialism bankrolled modern Scotland, but the stain of slavery and its architectural legacy, unlike the medieval fabric of St. Giles', cannot be easily scrubbed away.

Exploring Edinburgh features the best of the city's world heritage architecture; also historic sites and buildings in the hinterland where suburbs absorbed rural villages in the 19th and 20th centuries. The book's six tours are organised for walking, cycling, public transport or car. Entries are numbered and keyed to maps; many are near bus and tram stops. Each tour can be done in a day, longer at leisure. Buildings featured can be entered or viewed from the street. Each entry records the building's name, location, the architect(s) where known and the date of completion (and start dates where construction was lengthy). Artists, sculptors, structural engineers and landscape designers of interest are noted; also monuments and sculpture, especially in the city centre where, if you look up, 19th-century classical and Renaissance-style statues stare out from façades everywhere.

The World Heritage Site contains some 1,700 buildings of interest listed by Historic Environment Scotland. *Exploring Edinburgh* is a portable guide, so not all could be included. Those featured have been chosen variously for their social, cultural and political histories, and architectural quality. Modern buildings are noted, but not many because most are unworthy of the city and its World Heritage Site. Some buildings certified BREEAM (Building Research Establishment Environmental Assessment Methodology), meaning 'green', eco-friendly are featured. The Royal Incorporation of Architects in Scotland (RIAS) and other organisations give annual design awards; some of special interest are mentioned.

Doors Open Days, the annual opportunity to see inside buildings not normally open to the public, are recommended. Some properties are only open in season and not all are mobility-friendly (check their websites). Entries are indexed, not by page but by the entry numbers under which they can be found. The opening page of each tour lists those not to be missed.

—*Robin Ward*, Edinburgh 2020

The view from Castle Rock

Scotland's capital city is unique for its layers of historic buildings on a volcanic landscape eroded by an Ice Age glacier. No other city shows its social and topographical development as dramatically. There are panoramas, perspectives and sudden vistas – where turning a corner high up in the medieval Old Town will reveal the New Town, suburbia and the North Sea spread out like a map. An extinct volcano, Arthur's Seat, looms above everything.

This was the landscape Scottish monarchs beheld until the Union of the Crowns in 1603, when James VI became James I of England and moved the court from Holyrood Palace to London. Scotland's Parliament was dissolved in 1707 by the Act of Union, creating the British state. Scots lost their independence. Edinburgh became, in the words of poet Edwin Muir, 'a handsome, empty capital of the past'. The void was partly filled when the Scottish Parliament was revived in 1999. Its members meet in a landmark new building at the foot of the Royal Mile.

1

Holyrood & the Old Town

*Holyrood Abbey—Palace of Holyroodhouse—Scottish Parliament—
Canongate Tolbooth—Museum of Edinburgh—Moray House—Trinity Apse—The Scotsman Building—St Cecilia's Hall—Surgeons'
Hall—Old College—National Museum of Scotland—Greyfriars
Kirk—George Heriot's School—Central Library—The Grassmarket—
Edinburgh Castle—Scottish National War Memorial—Ramsay
Garden—Riddle's Close—The Writers' Museum—St Giles' High Kirk—
The Thistle Chapel . . .*

1

Holyrood Abbey

Palace of Holyroodhouse, Holyrood Park

Legend has it that King David I, deer-hunting in Holyrood Park, was attacked by a stag. He grabbed its antlers. They were transformed into a crucifix. To give thanks he founded in 1128 the Augustinian Abbey of Holyrood (Holy Cross). It was the most prestigious ecclesiastical structure in Scotland (twice the length of the ruin today). Excavations in 1911 proved the nave had been extended with a choir and north transept, and towers flanked the west door.

During the Wars of Independence, the abbey was looted by Edward II's army. In 1385, it was set ablaze – along with Holyrood Palace and the town – by Richard II, and desecrated again by the English in 1540s. The monastic regime was ousted during the Protestant Reformation of 1560. The grounds remained a sanctuary for debtors – cobblestones on Abbey Strand show where the boundary was; the crowstep-gabled building here (c. 1500) was an almshouse, originally perhaps the abbot's dwelling.

In 1633, the partly ruined abbey was repaired for the Scottish coronation of Charles I (the traceried east gable is from that time). James VII, the last Stuart monarch, made the nave the Chapel Royal, before he fled to exile in France in 1688. In 1758, it was roofed with stone slabs which collapsed ten years later. The wreckage was abandoned to erosion and decay, Victorian artists and writers were drawn to its sublime quality. It remains as they saw it.

2

Palace of Holyroodhouse
Horse Wynd, Holyrood Park

16th century; William Bruce 'Surveyor-general and overseer of the King's Buildings in Scotland' & Robert Mylne 'King's Master Mason' 1671–8

The official residence in Scotland of the reigning British monarch, who visits annually. Honours are granted. There is a garden party. But behind the ceremony and decorum there is a dark and bloody history.

Construction was started by James IV. James V added the double-barrelled North-west Tower, styled like a Loire château. It survived when Edinburgh was attacked by the English in the 1540s – the 'rough wooing', an attempt by Henry VIII to have his son Edward marry Mary Queen of Scots. She is the most romantic and ill-fated royal associated with Holyrood. It was here, in her apartments in the North-west Tower in 1566, that her private secretary David Rizzio was stabbed to death by assassins. A stain on the floor is said to be his blood.

In 1603, James VI became James I of England and took the Royal Court to London. The palace was revived by Charles II, who rebuilt it copying James V's tower to create a symmetrical west front. Its monumental Roman Doric gateway leads to a Renaissance-style courtyard. During the Jacobite rising of 1745, Bonnie Prince Charlie held court here. George IV, who visited the palace in 1822, ordered it be repaired and Queen Mary's apartments 'preserved sacred from every alteration'. King George is still here, dressed as a Highland chieftain in a portrait by David Wilkie in the Royal Dining Room. In the Long Gallery are portraits of Scottish monarchs, commissioned by Charles II.

The fountain in the forecourt is a Victorian replica of James V's original at Linlithgow Palace. The ornate gates (c. 1920), were part of a memorial to Edward VII, a statue of whom is in the forecourt. On Horse Wynd (the royal stables were here) is the Queen's Gallery (Benjamin Tindall Architects), a Victorian church and school converted to celebrate the Queen's Golden Jubilee 2002 and to exhibit artworks from the Royal Collection.

3

Scottish Parliament
Canongate and Horse Wynd

Enric Miralles & Benedetta Tagliabue (EMBT), RMJM architects, Arup engineers 2001–4

Scotland's old parliament 'voted itself out of existence' in 1707 when the Act of Union established the British Parliament in London. Repatriation of the Scottish Parliament was approved by referendum in 1997. An architectural competition was held, won by Barcelona-based EMBT. So loaded with political and cultural ambitions was the enterprise that it became as contentious as the dissolution almost three centuries before. Costs and criticism spiralled as the design evolved, but it was a masterpiece in the making. Architect Enric Miralles died before it was done.

The organic plan (seen in this aerial image) grows out of the Old Town – a 'dialogue across time' Miralles said. Leaf and boat shapes symbolise the land and sea of Scotland (the leaf motif inspired by the flower paintings of Charles Rennie Mackintosh). Spatial magic inside owes much to Antoni Gaudí. The office pods on the members' (MSP) block were conceived as 'monks' cells', to encourage the politicians to think. Queensberry House, a 17th-century mansion on the Canongate, was incorporated. Also on Canongate, the Canongate Wall, a concrete bulwark decorated with a collage of poetic quotations and stones from across the nation, and a sketch by Miralles of the Old Town.

The Debating Chamber is a luminous elliptical space under steel and glulam (glue-laminated) oak trusses, which recall the 17th-century roof of Old Parliament Hall (see entry 68). Craftsmanship and detailing throughout the building are exceptionally refined. Timber, concrete, steel and granite are the primary materials. The complex is sustainable, low-energy, rated BREEAM Excellent. There are green roofs and bee hives (the beeswax is used for official seals). The landscape, biodiverse with native plants and flowers, blends with historic Holyrood Park. Above all, the architecture dignifies parliament's purpose.

In 2005, the building won the Royal Institute of British Architects (RIBA) Stirling Prize and the Royal Incorporation of Architects in Scotland (RIAS) Andrew Doolan Award, respectively the top UK and Scottish architectural prizes.

4

Dynamic Earth
Holyrood Road at Holyrood Gait

Michael Hopkins & Partners 1999
Fabric-skinned pavilion looking like some prehistoric creature, lodged in the shell of a 19th-century brewery on the edge of Holyrood Park. The brewery walls, visible from Queen's Drive, were disguised as a castle to please Queen Victoria.

Dynamic Earth's style is High Tech, with the roof cable-stayed from steel pylons. Inside are exhibits about the evolution of Planet Earth. James Hutton, 'the founder of modern geology', lived nearby. Directly south are volcanic features that inspired him, Salisbury Crags and Arthur's Seat.

5

White Horse Close

27 Canongate

Looks like a film set but the buildings are real, restored in the 1960s (Frank Mears & Partners architects). The authors of *The Buildings of Scotland* judged this 'so blatantly fake that it can be acquitted of any intention to deceive.' The picturesque 17th-century form and style – forestairs, harled walls, crowstep gables and pantiled roofs – replicated Victorian reconstruction (c. 1890) for workers' housing by the Edinburgh Social Union, a philanthropic society created by Patrick Geddes (see 58).

The close was once famous for the White Horse Inn, a departure point for stagecoaches to London. During the Jacobite rising of 1745, Bonnie Prince Charlie's officers lodged here when the prince occupied the Palace of Holyroodhouse. The name refers to a white palfrey (a docile horse) said to have been the mount, stabled here, of Mary Queen of Scots.

6

Adam Smith's Panmure House

4 Lochend Close, Canongate

1691; EKJN Architects 2018

Built when the Canongate was a rural, aristocratic suburb of the Old Town. The name recalls the Earl of Panmure, a Jacobite who forfeited the property to the British state after the failed rising of 1715. In 1778, Adam Smith, author of *The Wealth of Nations*, moved in with his mother, cousin and nephew, and 3,000 books. Among those drawn to Smith's 'salons' were architect Robert Adam, chemist Joseph Black, geologist James Hutton and philosopher Dugald Stewart. Their spirit of enquiry inspired the restoration of the house by Heriot-Watt University as a forum for global economic and social debate.

7

Scottish Poetry Library

5 Crichton's Close, Canongate

Malcolm Fraser Architects 1999; Nicoll Russell Studios 2015

This was an award-winning building of exceptional clarity in an alley of

mixed-up buildings (tenements, an old brewery). Outdoor steps, like a medieval forestair, were used as seats for poetry readings, an informal interface with the public realm. Unfortunately this liberating feature was lost when the interior was enlarged by pushing the ground floor out to the property line.

8

112 Canongate

Richard Murphy Architects 1999

A Saltire Society Housing Design Award winner in 2000, designed for the Old Town Housing Association. Timber siding and harled walls evoke the past, along with upper rooms cantilevered from the façade to gain floor space, a form (see 17) familiar to residents of medieval Edinburgh. Script on the steel beam, 'A nation is forged in the hearth of poetry', alludes to instructive texts found on Old Town architecture (see 12) and to the Scottish Poetry Library down the close.

Across the street is Dunbar's Close Garden (Seamus Filor landscape design 1977). It was inspired by Patrick Geddes who advocated green spaces to bring nature to the Old Town's cramped closes where most people lived. The garden was donated by the Mushroom Trust to the city in 1978.

9

Canongate Kirk

153 Canongate

James Smith 1688–91

'Canongate' refers not to a gate, but *gait*, from the Norse word for 'street', where walked the canons of Holyrood Abbey. James VII ordered the kirk to be built for the congregation he evicted from the abbey, which he wanted for the Order of the Thistle (see 66). Funds were from monies left by merchant Thomas Moodie, noted on the façade which boasts a huge Dutch gable and

Roman Doric porch. The heraldry above the rose window represents William of Orange who took the British throne from James VII in 1688. The antlers on top of the gable recall the legend of King David's founding of Holyrood Abbey. The interior is festooned with royal and regimental banners and flags (this is the Kirk of Holyroodhouse and Edinburgh Castle).

10

Canongate Tolbooth

163 Canongate

Built in 1591, this was the town hall, court house and jail of the old Burgh of Canongate which was absorbed by Edinburgh in 1856. The style is Franco-Scottish – the architecture of the Auld Alliance (see 63). The forestair from the street led to the council chamber and court room. The jail was in the tower. The old burgh's Market (Mercat) Cross is in Canongate Kirkyard. Notable citizens buried here include Adam Smith and the prophet of the New Town, six-time Lord Provost George Drummond.

On the Tolbooth's façade is the burgh's coat of arms, dated 1128 when David I established Holyrood Abbey; also the stag that caused him to build it. Inscriptions in Latin read, 'Justice, piety, truth; thus is the way to the stars' and 'For Native Land and Posterity 1591.' Star and thistle finials appear above the Victorian attic windows; the clock on wrought iron brackets was installed in 1884; the tavern was established in 1820. The Tolbooth houses Edinburgh Museums' exhibition, The People's Story.

11

Robert Fergusson statue

Canongate

Robert Annand sculptor 2004

Competition-winning effigy of poet Fergusson, striding past Canongate Kirk. He died young in the city's Bedlam in 1774, alone except for his demons, and was buried in the kirkyard in an unmarked grave. Robert Burns, for whom Fergusson was an inspiration, found it 'unnoticed and unknown' in 1787 and paid for a headstone inscribed with an elegy he composed.

12

Museum of Edinburgh
140–146 Canongate
'The city's treasure box' is housed in several buildings, principally the gabled Huntly House, originally three adjoining timber structures, rebuilt in stone in 1570. The Latin inscriptions on the façade lent it a nickname, 'the talking house'. There were several successive owners, and a tenuous association with the Marquess of Huntly. The house was bought by the city in 1924 and restored as a museum (Frank Mears architect 1932). Its collection is illuminating, extensive and eccentric. An upgrade, reconfiguration and re-display (Benjamin Tindall Architects 2012) emphasised its serendipity.

Huntly House, Canongate Kirk and the Tolbooth form the largest cluster of 16th- and 17th-century urban buildings in Scotland. Among them is Acheson House in Bakehouse Close (146 Canongate). The close evokes the

past so well that location scouts for *Outlander* found it needed little dressing as a backdrop for the TV show's Jacobite setting. The original owner of the house was Archibald Acheson, a government minister for Charles I. In the courtyard is the Acheson crest (1633) – cockerel, trumpet, the motto 'Vigilantibus', meaning 'forever watchful', and a monogram with the initials of Archibald Acheson and his wife Margaret Hamilton.

In the 19th century, Bakehouse Close was a densely populated slum. At that time, Acheson House was a tenement and brothel, having been bought and sold several times, each transaction leading to decline. In 1924, it was bought by the city, sold to the 4th Marquess of Bute in 1935 and restored (Robert Hurd architect). Based here is Edinburgh World Heritage, for which the historic house was adapted (Benjamin Tindall Architects 2012).

13
Sugarhouse Close
154–166 Canongate, 41 Holyrood Road
18th century; rebuilt 1860s; Oberlanders Architects, Will Rudd Davidson engineers 2011–14

The name sounds sweet but hides the bitter taste of Scotland's role in the slave trade. The Edinburgh Sugar House Company opened a refinery here in 1752 (there were other refineries at the Port of Leith). The raw material came from plantations worked by African slaves in the West Indies. From 1829 to 1852, the refinery was owned by William Macfie & Co., the sugar dynasty established in 1788 at Greenock (Port Glasgow). Above the pend is a panel with the Clan Macfie lion rampant and motto 'Pro Rege', meaning 'For the King'.

When the site was redeveloped as a brewery in the 1860s, the Macfie panel, the two-storey oriel window in which it is set, and the crowstep gable with a star finial were evidently retained. Remains of the brewery have been blended into 'Sugarhouse Close', student accommodation expressed in varied built forms sympathetic in scale, materials and linear plan to the historic setting.

14
Moray House
174 Canongate
William Wallace master mason c. 1625

The finest of old Canongate's aristocratic townhouses, designed for the Countess of Home whose coat of arms is above the corbelled balcony on Canongate. In 1643, the house was inherited by her daughter, the Countess of Moray. It bristles with chimneys, crowstep gables and wrought iron gates with spiky pillars. Inside are original plaster ceilings and painted decoration. In 1848, Moray House became a school; later a college of education, absorbed by the University of Edinburgh in 1998.

The much-diminished garden originally extended to what is now Holyrood Road. Its Summer House has acquired notoriety. According to tradition, it was where the 'false and corrupted statesmen' who signed the 1707 Act of Union with England 'were obliged to hold their meetings in secret, lest

they should have been assaulted by the rabble' [of protesters]. So wrote Walter Scott in *Tales of a Grandfather*. Most Scots opposed the treaty but they had no vote. Robert Burns, in a poem of 1791, wrote that those who signed it had been bribed

and the nation 'sold for English gold'.

15

Bible Land

183–187 Canongate

1677

Tenement built for the Incorporation of Cordiners (shoemakers) of Canongate ('cordiner' from the French *courdouanier* meaning 'of Cordova', from where was imported the finest leather of the time). The cartouche above the door is finely decorated with carved cherub heads, the Green Man, a crown, a cordiner's leather-cutting knife, and an open book with an inscription from Psalm 133, hence 'Bible Land'. Another cordiners' plaque (1725) can been seen on Shoemakers' Land (195–197 Canongate).

These buildings, refurbished recently by Edinburgh World Heritage, are among several Canongate tenements reconstructed (Robert Hurd & Partners 1953–64). They include Morocco Land (265 Canongate). The figure of a Moor on its wall is said to recall fugitive Andrew Gray, sentenced to death for treason after the coronation of Charles I in 1633. He escaped to the Barbary Coast where he gained favour and wealth with the Sultan of Morocco. In 1645, Gray with a crew of corsairs sailed back to Edinburgh and threatened to sack the city. He secured a pardon by curing the Lord Provost's daughter of the plague, married her and settled here.

16
Tweeddale Court
14 High Street

Sixteenth-century courtyard, once the property of the Marquess of Tweeddale. It was a crime scene in 1806, when a British Linen Bank messenger was murdered and robbed of £4,000. The killer was not caught. The bank's building, Tweeddale House, is still here, complete with an Ionic-columned doorway. The name Oliver & Boyd above it recalls Edinburgh's distinguished history of printing and publishing.

Also in the courtyard is a fragment of the King's Wall, a fortification built by James II. Attached to it is the city's smallest heritage-listed building, an 18th-century lean-to used for storing sedan chairs on which the well-to-do could be carried so as not to set foot on the Old Town's filthy streets.

17
John Knox House
43–45 High Street

1470; enlarged c. 1560
John Knox is said to have lived here, an association which saved the house from demolition in the 19th century. In the 16th century, it was the home of Mariota Arres whose husband, James Mossman, was goldsmith to Mary Queen of Scots. Their initials are visible outside, along with a figure (Moses, not Knox), a sundial and a carved inscription 'Luve God abuve al and yi nychtbour as yi self.' Mossman's loyalty to the queen led to his execution in 1573.

Next door is Moubray House, mostly 17th century (earliest record 1477) with a forestair and overhanging gable, features once common. It was restored in 1910 by the Cockburn Association, which has an office in the cellars. Lord Henry Cockburn campaigned to prevent the Knox House being torn down. His spirit lives on in the association named after him. On the street outside is Netherbow Wellhead (William Bruce & Robert Mylne 1675).

The Knox House, a museum since 1853, is accessed from inside the

Scottish Storytelling Centre (Malcolm Fraser Architects, Elliott & Company engineers 2006), the world's first purpose built national centre for storytelling. On the wall is a plaque with the legend '1606, God save the King.' This is a relic of Netherbow Port, the most impressive of the Old Town's six gates. It was demolished in 1764 because it was too narrow for the increase in 'wheeled carriages' and pedestrian traffic. How it looked can be seen on a panel on the façade of the adjacent Victorian tenement. The clock from its tower was salvaged and later fitted to Dean Orphanage (see 135). Its bell, cast in the Netherlands in 1621, is housed in the Storytelling Centre's tower.

18
Heave Awa' House
Paisley Close, 101 High Street
John Rhind sculptor 1862

One night in 1861, a 16th-century tenement here collapsed, killing 35 of the 77 residents. In the pile of rubble the next morning, a boy's voice was heard by rescuers, 'Heave awa' lads, ah'm no' deid yet'. When the close was rebuilt, his release was honoured. His face, serene considering how he got here, is on the keystone. The tragedy and the hazardous condition of other tenements led to the City Improvement Act of 1867.

19
Trinity Apse
Chalmers Close
1462; reconstructed 1877

Trinity College Kirk was a unique relic of medieval Edinburgh. The North British Railway Company bought its site from the city to build Waverley Station and, in 1848, the kirk was dismantled – 'scandalous desecration', Henry Cockburn thundered. Its stones were numbered and stored for re-erection, to be paid for by the NBR.

Proposals to rebuild it on Calton Hill, Castle Rock or in Princes Street Gardens came and went. Other builders helped themselves to the stockpile, leaving 'a medieval jigsaw puzzle'. In 1877, the remaining stones were used to reconstruct the apse, attached to a new church at the foot of Chalmers Close.

When that church was demolished in 1964, the apse was spared. It remains a wonder of medieval masons' craft, lofty and fan-vaulted. Numbered stones can be still be spotted. The south wall faces a garden where a few stones not re-erected are scattered – gargoyles, a monster's feet, the Green Man.

A 15th-century altarpiece painted by Hugo van der Goes for the original kirk is in the National Gallery.

20

Old St Paul's Scottish Episcopal Church
Jeffrey Street and Carruber's Close

Hay & Henderson 1883

Two Gothic gables, one with a sculpture of Christ on the cross, conceal one of the city's finest ecclesiastical interiors. There is a door in the close, or you can enter from the street and climb the Calvary Stair to the nave. Either way, you enter a timber-roofed, richly decorated sanctuary. Among its treasures are reredos with painted panels like Florentine frescoes and a trio of stained glass windows depicting Saint Paul, The Crucifixion and Saint Columba. The War Memorial Chapel (1926) displays the Martyrs' Cross, a small iron cross that hung opposite the gallows on the Grassmarket. It was the last thing seen by the condemned – among them some members of the congregation (Scottish Episcopalians were persecuted for supporting the Jacobite risings of 1715 and 1745). Also in the chapel is a haunting artwork, *Still* (Alison Watt 2004).

21

The Scotsman Building
North Bridge

Dunn & Findlay architects, Redpath, Brown & Co. engineers 1900–4

Once the beating heart of *The Scotsman* newspaper's empire. The masthead shines on the north façade. The thistle was chosen as the emblem not only because it is Scotland's national plant but also because it is spiky and sharp, as the paper's founders set out to be in 1817. They campaigned for political and civic reform. The office was in Craig's Close; later at 26–30 Cockburn Street (Peddie & Kinnear 1860), before the paper relocated to this 'pagoda of publishing excellence'.

Allegorical sculptures of Mercury the messenger, Night and Day (after Michelangelo) and Peace animate the stonework. The building's co-designer, James Leslie Findlay, was the younger son of John Ritchie Findlay, the paper's publisher. The architecture was described in a promotional booklet as 'Free Renaissance style with French château features'. Very free: the effect is baroque. The historicism concealed an 11-storey, steel-framed vertically organised complex. A lavishly decorated lobby (in situ), editorial offices and the newsroom were at North Bridge; below were composing (typesetting) and the press room where the paper was printed; dispatch was on Market Street. In 1998, the owners of *The Scotsman* sold the building. It is now The Scotsman Hotel (the masthead on the façade had to be kept as part of the building's heritage).

The Scotsman Steps (Dunn & Findlay c. 1900) link North Bridge with Market Street in a tower derived from the spiral staircase at the Château Royal de Blois. The tower was restored by the city and Edinburgh World Heritage in 2011. The steps were re-surfaced as public art (Martin Creed artist) with marble sourced from around the world; commissioned by the Fruitmarket Gallery.

North Bridge was built to provide a direct link from the Old Town to Leith, and to the New Town anticipated by Lord Provost George Drummond, who laid the foundation stone for the bridge in 1763 (the present structure dates from 1897; bronze plaques on the parapets note its history). The Scotsman Building and the former Patrick Thomson's department store (also now a hotel) were constructed at the south end of the bridge. They act like a proscenium framing the Old Town's theatre of street life. The urban design was borrowed from an unrealised neoclassical scheme by Robert Adam.

22

North Bridge Arcade

North Bridge and Cockburn Street

Dunn & Findlay c. 1900

A shortcut between Cockburn Street and North Bridge modelled on the 19th-century *passages* of Paris. The ceiling has starry mosaics, and there is a classical rotunda with an Art Nouveau coloured glass dome. All original, an echo of past elegance.

23

Fleshmarket Close

Connects the Royal Mile to Market Street. It was named for the Flesh Market – the meat market and slaughterhouse at the foot of the close before Waverley Station was built (the fruit, vegetable and fish markets were there too). It was bisected in the 1860s by Cockburn Street, but remains steep, dark and claustrophobic, a good place to dump bodies. Ian Rankin thought so: two skeletons are found here in *Fleshmarket Close*, one of his Detective Rebus stories.

24

Fruitmarket Gallery

45 Market Street

1938; Richard Murphy Architects 1993

The gallery opened in 1974 in this former market building, later refreshed with a butterfly-roofed intervention by Richard Murphy. Part of the front façade was taken out for an entrance to the gallery, shop and café. Exhibition space is at the back and upstairs. The staircase can be raised to let large artworks in; for the upper floor, there is a hoist, intriguingly visible from the street. Clerestories and new windows provided views of the city, visually connecting the gallery to its urban context. The building is supported on a huge steel girder where it backs onto Waverley Station, from where produce was transferred.

In 2020, the gallery was extended (Reiach & Hall Architects) into the building next door, originally a fruit and vegetable warehouse.

25
City Art Centre
2 Market Street

Dunn & Findlay c. 1900

Big-city Edwardian baroque block, originally part of *The Scotsman* newspaper's complex. It was retrofitted in 1980 for the city's collection of Scottish art. The leading edge of the first floor was cut back to create a double-height foyer. A lively mural (William Crosbie artist) decorates the café.

26
Waverley Cafe
Market Street at Waverley Bridge

Ebenezer James McRae, City Architect c. 1930

Dozens of police telephone boxes like this were produced for the city at the Carron Foundry, Falkirk. The cast iron boxes are unique to Edinburgh's townscape, which inspired their classical style. Many have been sold and retrofitted as coffee outlets or pop-up arts venues. All were originally painted police blue. This is one of several heritage-listed by Historic Environment Scotland.

27
Royal Edinburgh Military Tattoo
Offices
1 Cockburn Street

Peddie & Kinnear 1860; Malcolm Fraser Architects, Calum Duncan Architects 2016

Cockburn Street was named for advocate, judge and conservationist Henry Cockburn. He is commemorated with a profile relief above the entrance to the former Cockburn Hotel (the faded name 'Macpherson' on the lintel probably refers to an early proprietor). The street was constructed to connect Waverley Station with the Royal Mile. It snakes up to ease the climb. It is picturesque. The Edinburgh Railway Station Access Act of 1853 required that the buildings (most by Peddie

& Kinnear) should 'preserve as far as possible the architectural style and antique character of the locality'. In the fashion of the time, that meant Scots Baronial. In 2013, the Cockburn Hotel building was acquired by the Tattoo organisation for which it was refurbished.

28

The Tron Kirk

122 High Street

> *John Mylne master mason; John Scott master*
> *wright 1636–47; Richard & Robert Dickson*
> *1828*

Presbyterians displaced when Charles I declared St Giles' High Kirk a cathedral received this compensation from the king. The name is from the 'tron', a public weigh beam for salt and other commodities once nearby. Below the kirk are archaeological remains of Marlin's Wynd, the earliest paved street in Scotland. Two sides of the kirk were removed (c. 1785) for South Bridge and Hunter Square. During the Great Fire of 1824, the kirk was showered with flying embers which destroyed the Dutch-style timber and lead-clad bell tower. The façades and hammerbeam roof were spared, and the tower rebuilt in stone.

Worship ceased in 1952. The kirk became a Hogmanay and Festival Fringe venue. Edinburgh World Heritage recently leased it from the city for conservation. A timber vestibule respectful of the oak-roofed heritage was installed (Oliver Chapman Architects 2018); also an exhibit by EWH about the Old and New Towns and Scotland's other World Heritage Sites.

29

Radisson Blu Hotel

80 High Street

Ian Begg Architects 1990

Tenement housing with traditional Old Town closes and back courts was planned for what was a gap site here. Didn't happen. The Scandic Crown Hotel (now the Radisson Blu) did, disguised as a tenement in Scots Baronial style. The façades were varied to visibly reduce the bulk of what is a very big modern building inside. They feature rubble stone and coloured render; there are pitched roofs, gables and dormer windows, and turreted drum towers that look like they walked up the Royal Mile from Holyroodhouse. The Danish client 'wanted a building of strong character and it had to make clear that it was in Scotland – people visiting had to be in no doubt where they were'. Lest anyone be deceived by its antique appearance, the date of completion is on a plaque at the Niddry Street corner.

30
St Cecilia's Hall
50 Niddry Street

Robert Mylne 1763; Page\Park Architects, David Narro Associates engineers 2017
Scotland's oldest concert hall, built for the Edinburgh Musical Society and named after the patron saint of musicians. Its intimate, oval-shaped concert room was a fashionable venue in the Old Town until South Bridge blighted the neighbourhood. Concert-goers deserted St Cecilia's for the Assembly Rooms in the New Town (see 107).

St Cecilia's became successively a Baptist church, a Freemasons lodge, a school, and a 1930s dance hall. It was restored in the 1960s (Ian Lindsay & Partners) to house the University of Edinburgh's collection of historic musical instruments. Recent refurbishment has increased awareness of the collection and access to it. A musical metaphor was irresistible – the parrot and flower patterns on the bronze screen above the entrance were inspired by the decoration on a Georgian double-keyboard harpsichord displayed inside.

South Bridge (1785–8) spans Cowgate ravine on multiple arches. It looked like a Roman aqueduct until hidden by tenements and shops. Only the arch above the Cowgate remains exposed. The arches, known as South Bridge Vaults, were workshops or storage for businesses above. The mysterious underworld is still there, abandoned and said to be haunted. After the bridge was built, the Cowgate became a slum. Robert Louis Stevenson writing *Edinburgh, Picturesque Notes* observed, 'To look over the South Bridge and see the Cowgate below full of crying hawkers, is to view one rank of society from another in the twinkling of an eye.'

31
St Patrick's Church
5 South Gray's Close, Cowgate
John Baxter 1771–4; Reginald Fairlie 1929
Originally called Cowgate Chapel, built for Scottish
Episcopalians who, at the time, were subject to
penal laws for supporting the Jacobites. Ministers
who took an oath recognising the Hanoverian
monarchy were permitted to preach. Architect Baxter's design echoed
St Martin-in-the-Fields in London, until overlaid in 1929 with a grandiose
neoclassical façade. Interior decoration included a mural, *The Ascension of
the Lord*, by Alexander Runciman.

In 1818, after the congregation moved to the New Town, the church was
sold to the United Presbyterians who, shunning iconography, over-painted
the mural. The Catholic Church bought the building in 1856, to serve
Highlanders and Irish who migrated to Edinburgh to escape poverty (many
others settled in Glasgow). In 2018, the mural, the earliest artwork in a Scottish church since the Reformation, was uncovered for restoration.

32
**Edinburgh Centre for Carbon
Innovation (ECCI)**
High School Yards, Infirmary Street
Malcolm Fraser Architects 2013
High School Yards, part of the Uni-
versity of Edinburgh, was the site of
Black Friars Dominican Priory and, subsequently, the Royal High School. The
school's building of 1777 (Alexander Laing architect) still stands. Walter Scott
was a pupil (the initials 'WS' on the Roman Doric porch might have been
scratched by him). When the school moved to Calton Hill in 1829, the building was sold to the Royal Infirmary, which needed more space. The original
Infirmary building (William Adam 1742) was demolished after the hospital
moved to Lauriston Place in 1870 (see 157). Its gates were saved and can be
seen at the Drummond Street entrance to High School Yards.

The former High School building is now the Centre for Carbon Innovation,
for research to combat climate change. The extension on Surgeons' Square

is wood-framed with cross-laminated timber (CLT), a sustainable material of choice. The retrofit and extension was the first such intervention to a heritage-listed building in the UK to be rated BREEAM Outstanding.

33

Dovecot Studios

10 Infirmary Street

Robert Morham, City Architect 1887; Malcolm Fraser Architects, Elliott & Company engineers 2009

Tapestry weaving workshop in a luminous, galleried space, formerly Infirmary Street Baths, the first public facility of its type in the city. The pool was floored over but the original volume, timber roof and Victorian façade were retained. There is exhibition space, a shop and café. The studios were founded by the 4th Marquess of Bute in 1912, inspired by William Morris and the Arts and Crafts movement. The name is from the Doocot at Corstorphine (see 284) where the studios were first established.

34

Rutherford's Bar

3 Drummond Street

Original teak wood-fronted bar of 1834 favoured by Robert Louis Stevenson when he was at the University of Edinburgh studying engineering, later law. He was a president of the Speculative Society, a literary and debating club. Formal meetings over, RLS and his chums would repair to Rutherford's. In 2007, the bar was revamped as the 'Hispaniola', the name of the schooner on which the hero of *Treasure Island* sets sail.

35

Festival Theatre

13-29 Nicolson Street

William & Thomas Milburn 1928; Law & Dunbar-Nasmith 1994

There have been theatres on this site since the 1820s. The most lavish was the Empire

Palace of 1892, an Aladdin's cave of gilded décor until gutted by fire in 1911. It was rebuilt in 1928 with a more muted but still impressive auditorium, which became a bingo hall in the 1960s. In 1994, it was returned to theatre use. The project incorporated a new stage extension and fly tower, back of house facilities and a new, glazed foyer building. There is of course a ghost – illusionist Sigmund Neuberger, stage name 'The Great Lafayette', whose act caused the fire of 1911 in which he perished.

36
Surgeons' Hall and Museum
Nicolson Street
William Playfair 1832

The Royal College of Surgeons of Edinburgh was incorporated in 1505 in the Old Town. In 1697, the surgeons moved to High School Yards, subsequently to this Greek Revival temple to their status. Among past presidents of the college was surgeon and professor Joseph Bell, famous for powers of observation and deduction, the inspiration for Arthur Conan Doyle's Sherlock Holmes.

The museum was originally a resource for medical students. Its most notorious member of staff was curator and anatomy teacher Robert Knox. His need of bodies for dissection led William Burke and William Hare to supply them, by murder. The story is well known; less so that Burke's body was dissected by a member of the college and that his death mask is among the macabre curiosities here.

37
Old College
South Bridge
Robert Adam 1789–93; William Playfair 1816–27; Robert Rowand Anderson (dome) 1887

No building symbolises better the University of Edinburgh's role since 1583 in the city's cultural and intellectual life than Robert Adam's stupendous and scholarly set piece on South Bridge. The six colossal columns on the portico were extracted from Craigleith Quarry. Each weighed nine tons and was

nine metres long. They were hauled by horses to the construction site and erected. Above them, the architect's name is inscribed on a commemorative panel in Roman style (Adam, like many architects and artists of the time, made a pilgrimage to Italy to study the relics of the classical world). The Doric columns flank a vaulted triumphal archway which leads to a quadrangle with neoclassical façades on all sides. On the dome is the 'Golden Boy' holding the Torch of Knowledge (John Hutchison sculptor).

The quad was completed by William Playfair after Adam died. It has been restored, after years as a car park, to fulfil Playfair's vision of an area of grass surrounded by paving (Simpson & Brown Architects 2011). The work revealed (and then concealed) an extraordinarily rich archaeology beneath the quad. On the north side is the Law School (refurbished LDN Architects 2018). On the south side is the majestic, barrel-vaulted Playfair Library. At the far end of the library is the Talbot Rice Gallery of contemporary art. The gallery's Georgian Room was originally the university's Natural History Museum (see 191).

Nearby, outside the National Museum on Chambers Street (next entry), is the Playfair Monument with the architect, portfolio in hand, beside a stumpy Doric column (Alexander Stoddart sculptor 2016). He faces a statue of publisher and Lord Provost William Chambers (John Rhind sculptor 1891) who restored St Giles' (see 65) and planned Chambers Street to bring civic space and light into this part of the Old Town.

38

National Museum of Scotland

Chambers Street

Two museums, merged in 2006: the Royal Scottish Museum (Captain Francis Fowke & Robert Matheson 1861–89) and the Museum of Scotland (Benson & Forsyth Architects 1995–8).

The Royal Scottish Museum was established in 1854 as the Industrial Museum of Scotland and built in three phases. Its design owes much to the Palais de l'Industrie at the 1855 Paris World Fair, which Captain Fowke, a Royal Engineer, attended as a British representative. The French building had a Beaux-Arts frontage and an iron and glass hall influenced by the Crystal Palace (1851) in London. The Royal Museum has a similar hall, behind a Venetian Renaissance façade where sculptural groups represent Science (flanked by Textile Manufacturing and Engineering), Natural History and Applied Art (John Rhind sculptor c. 1888); also portrait medallions of Victoria and Albert, Darwin, Michelangelo, Newton and Watt. There is no better example in Edinburgh of the Victorian personality caught between contemporary engineering and the architecture of the past.

Refurbishment (Gareth Hoskins Architects, David Narro Associates engineers 2008–11) decluttered the hall, rationalised circulation and redisplayed the collections throughout. The hall is now approached from a vaulted undercroft. The ascent and sudden encounter with Fowke's luminous space is one of Edinburgh's most memorable architectural moments.

There is an internal link to the former Museum of Scotland – its original entrance is the drum-shaped tower, like a castle from the mists of time. The building is a puzzle of architectural references, among them the Soane Museum in London, and the sculptural forms of Le Corbusier featured on the roof. The interior is labyrinthine, layered like the Old Town, filled with weird and wonderful objects. The roof garden is planted to represent Scottish natural habitats; panoramic view too. The overall design was nominated for

the Royal Institute of British Architects (RIBA) Stirling Prize 1999. The renewal of the former Royal Scottish Museum won the Royal Incorporation of Architects in Scotland (RIAS) Andrew Doolan Award, Best Building in Scotland 2011.

39
The Watt Institution Building
25 Chambers Street
David Cousin & David Rhind 1872; John Chessar 1888
The Watt Institution was a technical college, originally the Edinburgh Mechanics' Institute (founded in 1821; the first of its type in the world). The Mechanics' building was demolished when Chambers Street was constructed c. 1870. This replacement was commissioned by the Watt Institution, aided by George Heriot's Trust. The sculpture of a boy with a hammer and anvil high above the entrance represents crafts and industry.

The Watt Institution, now Heriot-Watt University, was named in 1851 after engineer and inventor James Watt. A statue of him (1854) originally here is at Heriot-Watt's Riccarton Campus. The Chambers Street building has French-style façades, mansard roofs and decorative ironwork dating from reconstruction in 1888. In 1990, it was converted for the Crown Office and Procurator Fiscal Service, part of the Sheriff Court complex.

40
Greyfriars Kirk
Greyfriars Place
1620
The first kirk on this site was barn-like, with a chunky tower for which a spire was planned. The tower collapsed in 1718 when gunpowder stored inside by the Town Guard exploded. The church was reconstructed in 1721 for two congregations, Old and New

Greyfriars. The doors for each were in the Palladian porch on the north side, now the main entrance. The tower did not rise again.

Old Greyfriars, east-facing with a baroque gable, was gutted by fire in 1845 and New Greyfriars damaged. Reconstruction by a progressive minister, Robert Lee, included the first coloured glass in a Presbyterian church in the city since the Reformation, and a pipe organ (music and decoration were scorned by joyless hard-line Presbyterians). After the kirk reverted to a single congregation in 1929, the Gothic aisles lost in the fire were reinstated (Henry Francis Kerr c.1935) and the building given a single-span Californian red-wood roof. A fascinating museum records the history of the kirk. The name is from a Franciscan (Greyfriars) friary here until the Reformation. Among the kirk's relics is an original copy of the National Covenant, signed here in 1638 to oppose Charles II's 'divine right' to obstruct Presbyterian worship and religious freedom.

41

Greyfriars Kirkyard
Greyfriars Place
16th century
When the burial ground at St Giles' High Kirk filled up, Mary Queen of Scots, in 1562, allowed the town council to lay out this 'theatre of mortality' on the site of Greyfriars Friary, which was sacked during the Reformation. Eroded angels, skeletons and skulls whisper to the living on Candlemaker Row – others stare from memorials that loom in ruinous classical grandeur, like the monument (shown above) to advocate James Chalmers by master mason Robert Mylne (1675). Architect William Adam's family mausoleum (1753), designed by his sons Robert and John, is here; also the grave, origi-nally unmarked, of James Craig, designer of the New Town Plan (a memorial stone was laid by the Saltire Society in the 1930s).

There is a section of the Flodden Wall, built to defend Edinburgh after the Scots were defeated at the Battle of Flodden in 1513. Here too is the Martyrs' Monument (1709, enlarged 1771). It acknowledges the 1,000 or so

Covenanters imprisoned in the kirkyard following their capture by royalist forces at the Battle of Bothwell Bridge in 1679. Those who refused to swear allegiance to Charles II were executed or exiled by King's Advocate George 'Bluidy' Mackenzie whose soul, as Robert Louis Stevenson put it, 'is certainly in hell'. His uneasy spirit lingers in the Mackenzie Mausoleum which he commissioned before he died in 1691. The classical, domed rotunda (James Smith architect) is the most sinister piece of architecture in Edinburgh. Poltergeist reported. Ghost tours advertised.

42

Greyfriars Bobby

George IV Bridge at Candlemaker Row

William Brodie sculptor 1873

Bronze sculpture of the legendary Skye terrier that kept a 14-year vigil by his master's grave in Greyfriars Kirkyard. When the town council decreed stray dogs be caught and killed, William Chambers bought Bobby a collar, inscribed 'Greyfriars Bobby from the Lord Provost, 1867. Licensed.' Bobby was buried in the kirkyard in 1872. His collar is in the Museum of Edinburgh (see 12).

43

George Heriot's School

Lauriston Place

William Wallace 1628–59

George Heriot was goldsmith to James VI, whom he followed to London in 1603. On his death in 1624, he left money for a 'hospital' (meaning school and orphanage) for 'faitherless bairns'.

The Scottish Renaissance-style school (seen here on the skyline from Victoria Terrace; see 47) was built around a quadrangle, with the principal façade facing the Old Town. Its architect, William Wallace, Master Mason to the Scottish Crown, died in 1631. He was succeeded by his assistant, William Aytoun. The building was requisitioned in 1650 by Cromwell for use as an army hospital. The school opened in 1659; clock tower completed in the 1690s (Robert Mylne master mason); sculpture of Heriot (1645) in the quad.

Access today is from Lauriston Place. The Gatehouse (1828), like a miniature model of the school, was designed by William Playfair who also landscaped the grounds. In 1833, the school's original rubble-stone outer walls (on the east, west and south elevations) were refaced with ashlar (Alexander Black, architect for Heriot's Trust) to match the north frontage.

Fans of JK Rowling's Harry Potter books have been heard to exclaim, on seeing the school's turrets, 'Hogwarts!' The author began writing the stories in Edinburgh and several sites have been identified as inspiration for them.

44

Augustine United Church
41 George IV Bridge

William Hardie Hay & James Murdoch Hay 1861
Eclectic Romanesque and Renaissance design with a triple-tiered tower as if from a fairy tale. Structural instability was fixed by architect David Bryce who fitted cast iron columns to support the timber roof and gallery. Built for members of the Congregational Church whose previous chapel was demolished to make way for the Royal Scottish Museum (see 38).

45

Central Library
George IV Bridge

George Washington Browne
1887–90
A people's palace styled like French Renaissance château. Above the entrance are the words 'Let there be Light', the motto of Scottish-American steel baron Andrew Carnegie who laid the foundation stone. He said free public libraries were a 'cradle of democracy' and funded more than 2,500 worldwide (the first was built in 1883 in his home town, Dunfermline). There is a bust of Carnegie (Charles McBride sculptor) in a niche on the staircase, the way up to the domed, galleried Reference Library on the top floor.

Next door is the Art & Design Library, formerly the Fine Art Library of

1936. Originally, this was the Highland and Agricultural Society of Scotland's museum (John Henderson c. 1839). In 1855, its contents were transferred to the newly created Industrial Museum (see 38) and the building became the society's offices. Above the door is a tableau with Caledonia blessing a kilted reaper and ploughboy (Alexander Handyside Ritchie sculptor 1840). The inscription in Latin means 'Always armed and now industrious', conceivably a reference to the taming of the Highlanders after the Jacobite rising of 1745 and the subsequent agricultural 'improvements' commonly known as the Clearances. The society is now known for the annual Royal Highland Show.

46
National Library of Scotland
George IV Bridge
Reginald Fairlie 1934–6; 1950–6
Steel-framed, stone-clad box much larger than it looks – below street level there are seven floors of storage for millions of books, manuscripts and other printed material. It is Scotland's largest reference library, established in 1925 to house the historic collection of the Advocates Library given to the nation. Completion was delayed by the Second World War. Art Deco statues on the façade (Hew Lorimer sculptor) symbolise Medicine, Science, History, Literature, Law, Theology and Music. Traditional foyer; top-lit Reading Room in 1930s classical style.

47
Victoria Street
Thomas Hamilton 1829–34
Plunging streetscape with Victoria Terrace on a raised promenade, planned after the City Improvement Act of 1827; another act followed in 1867. Both were passed by council to sweep away slums. Victoria Street replaced much of Brodie's Close (see 61) and most of West Bow, a steep zigzag wynd between the Royal Mile and the Grassmarket.

48

Magdalen Chapel

41 Cowgate

c. 1540

Funded by a bequest which assigned patronage to the Incorporation of Hammermen, the trade guild for blacksmiths and other metalworkers. Attached to the chapel were an almshouse and chaplain's dwelling. The tower was added in 1622. On a plaque above the entrance is the guild's crown and hammer motif and the founders' emblem. In the Convening Hall is the Deacon's Chair of 1708 and four heraldic stained glass roundels, the only pre-Reformation stained glass in Scotland in its original location.

The arch over the Cowgate is George IV Bridge (c. 1830), multi-arched, most of it hidden by later buildings. It was designed by architect Thomas Hamilton, following the 1827 City Improvement Act.

49

The Grassmarket

Established in 1477 at the west end of the Cowgate, by a royal charter issued by James III. Horses and cattle were traded at fairs: the 'grass' in the name refers to fodder in their pens. 'Cowgate' was the name of a drovers' trail. There was a corn exchange for merchants, along with shops, inns and taverns. The Black Bull is named for a howff where workers and traders drank.

This being the Old Town, there are ghosts aplenty. In 1736, a rowdy crowd at the hanging of a notorious but popular smuggler was fired upon by the Town Guard. Nine citizens were shot dead and 18 wounded. The Captain of the Guard, John Porteous, was charged with murder and held in a cell at the Tolbooth. When word got out that he was to be given a royal pardon from London, the mob reassembled. Porteous was dragged to the Grassmarket and lynched. He was buried in Greyfriars Kirkyard.

During the 'killing times' of the 17th century, 100 Covenanters were executed here (a stone circle marks the spot). The White Hart Inn, founded in 1516, said to be the oldest in Edinburgh, was frequented by murderers Burke and Hare (see 36); the inn's name is thought to refer to the legend of King David and the stag and the founding of Holyrood Abbey.

At the east end of the Grassmarket is one of the Old Town's surviving well-heads (1674; restored 1861). At the west end is West Port, named for one of the city gates in the 16th-century Flodden Wall. Part of the wall is in the Vennel, the steep alley to Lauriston Place; another section is inside Dance Base.

50
Dance Base
14-16 Grassmarket
Malcolm Fraser Architects 2001
Dance Base was planned ingeniously to fit a precipitous site below Edinburgh Castle. The entrance, through the pend next door to the Black Bull tavern, lures you up through the layered complex, each transition defined by activity and architectural use of timber, concrete, steel and glass. Clerestory windows in the studios and opaque structural floor-glass allow daylight to penetrate most parts of the facility. A rubble-stone relic of the Flodden Wall lines the west side of a corridor that connects the reception area to roof decks and Studio 3, a perfectly proportioned Zen-like room with a pyramidal roof and central oculus. Magical.

Dance Base won the inaugural RIAS Andrew Doolan Award, Best Building in Scotland 2002 and was a Stirling Prize finalist that year.

51

Edinburgh Castle

Castlehill, The Royal Mile

William Wallace and Robert the Bruce, heroes of the Wars of Independence, guard the gate to Edinburgh Castle. The bronze statues – Wallace (Alexander Carrick sculptor) on the north side of the archway and Bruce (Thomas Clapperton) on the south side – were unveiled in 1929. Above is the Royal Standard and a banner with the Latin *Nemo Me Impune Lacessit*, 'No one attacks me with impunity', the motto of Scottish monarchs.

Castle Rock has been occupied since prehistoric times, and the castle besieged, burned and rebuilt over the centuries. The most daring exploit was its capture in 1314 by the Earl of Moray, who led a band of patriots up Castle Rock at night by secret route and seized it from the English garrison. The most formidable fortification is the 16th-century Half Moon Battery, named for its shape. In 1745, Bonnie Prince Charlie's Jacobite army failed to capture the fortress, the final time it was attacked.

There is an array of royal and military structures: among them the 12th-century Queen Margaret's Chapel, the oldest building in Edinburgh; the Royal Palace and Great Hall (both 16th century), the National War Museum and the National War Memorial. The Great Hall was built by James IV for ceremonies and banquets. Its timber hammer beam roof is original; décor fanciful, Victorian. The palace contains the Honours of Scotland – the crown, sceptre and sword of state first used together in 1543 for the coronation of Mary Queen of Scots. Here, too, is the Stone of Destiny on which Scottish monarchs were crowned.

The castle is approached from the Esplanade, a windy 18th-century parade ground flanked with memorials from an era when kilted Highlanders were the shock troops of the British Empire. Their successors, serving with the Royal Regiment of Scotland, are more likely to be seen performing at the Edinburgh Military Tattoo, held on the Esplanade since 1950. Victorian resto-

rations – which started in the 1850s at Queen Margaret's Chapel (at the time a gunpowder store) – accelerated the citadel's transformation from an army barracks to the historic attraction it is today. The gateway Wallace and Bruce guard admits over 2 million visitors a year.

52
Scottish National War Memorial
Edinburgh Castle
Robert Lorimer 1923–7

Spectacular First World War memorial astride the highest point on Castle Rock. The Duke of Atholl raised support to campaign for it. It was created of the idea that Scotland should have its own commemoration, not simply be attached to a British one proposed (but not built) for Hyde Park in London.

Architect Robert Lorimer, chosen by competition, visualised a 'sturdy, massive type of Scotch Gothic with external buttresses rising out of the rock'. An image showing how it would 'vandalise' the castle's skyline was published in *The Scotsman*. Critics fired warning shots. The committee overseeing the project retreated. Lorimer reworked the design to incorporate an 18th-century barracks block, which he remodelled in Scottish Renaissance style inspired by the royal palace at Stirling Castle.

In niches on the façade are eight symbolic statues. Flanking the entrance are the Scottish unicorn and the English lion. Above the door are a phoenix and a sombre sculpture, 'The Survival of the Spirit'. Inside is the Hall of Honour, a neoclassical space where Lorimer deployed a battalion of artists and artisans to create sculptures, friezes and stained glass illustrating Scottish regiments, nurses, sailors and airmen – even the animals and carrier pigeons used by the forces. It was the most ambitious programme of public art in Edinburgh since the National Portrait Gallery was built (see 91).

The artistic and emotional apogee is The Shrine, a Gothic apse where stands a casket containing the Rolls of Honour which list by name the dead. Suspended above it is an oak carving of God's soldier, the Archangel Michael, expressing, as was hoped at the time, 'mankind's triumph over the evil of war'. Most evocative of time and memory is Castle Rock itself, part of which is exposed on the floor of The Shrine.

**53
Cannonball
House
Castlehill**
At the top of the Royal Mile is a tenement gable-end with a cannonball stuck in the stonework. Legend has it that the ball was fired by the castle's gunners at Bonnie Prince Charlie's Jacobite army in 1745.

Another explanation is that the ball was placed to mark the elevation of Comiston Springs, five kilometres south, the source of the city's first reliable water supply. Pipes were laid by a Dutch engineer hired by the town council following a Scottish Parliament Act in 1621 'to bring the sweet waters of the country to the centre of Edinburgh'. The water was stored in Castlehill Reservoir, a cavernous cistern which supplied public wellheads still standing at the

Grassmarket, the High Street and Netherbow. The reservoir, rebuilt in 1850, was drained in 1992 and repurposed as the Tartan Weaving Mill.

54
Ramsay Garden
Ramsay Lane

> *Stewart Henbest Capper, Sydney Mitchell & Wilson 1893*

A bonny block of Arts and Crafts apartments commissioned by Patrick Geddes. It seems to defy the topography, stepping deftly down towards Princes Street Gardens. The façade shown here faces Castle Esplanade. The Geddes family flat was on the fourth floor. The complex was designed primarily to provide accommodation for staff and students at the University of Edinburgh. Geddes revived several tenements in the Old Town for that purpose. At Ramsay Garden, he incorporated the house of poet Allan Ramsay (see 102).

Geddes invited artist John Duncan to decorate many of Ramsay Garden's rooms, with murals of Celtic myths and landscapes. Duncan also designed Witches Well, the Art Nouveau drinking fountain set in the wall by the Esplanade. It recalls folk accused of witchcraft who were burned at the stake here in the 16th and 17th centuries.

55
Outlook Tower
Castlehill

A 17th-century tenement reconstructed in 1853 to look like a castle for Maria Short, daughter of Thomas Short who founded the first observatory on Calton Hill (see 73). Maria built her own observatory on the hill. It was popular. The town council thought it an eyesore and evicted her. Undaunted, she opened Maria Short's Observatory here. Patrick Geddes bought it in 1892, renamed it Outlook Tower and opened a museum and centre for urban studies. Later, the building was part of the University of Edinburgh. It is now the Camera Obscura and World of Illusions. The camera obscura, in the tower's octagonal belvedere, was the main attraction in the observatory Maria Short built.

56

The Hub

Castlehill

> *James Gillespie Graham & Augustus Welby Pugin 1839–44; Benjamin Tindall Architects 1999*

Tremendous structure with pinnacles and a 73-metre high steeple, briefly Edinburgh's tallest (see 167). The design of the steeple was intended by Pugin for, but not added to, St George's Southwark in London.

Opened as Victoria Hall, the Gothic Revival building has accommodated the General Assembly of the Church of Scotland and congregations since merged with Greyfriars Kirk (see 40). In 1929, the assembly moved across Castlehill to the former Free Church Hall (built in 1859 on the site of the palace of Mary of Guise, mother of Mary Queen of Scots). Victoria Hall became Highland Tolbooth St John's Church, where worshipped Gaelic- and English-speaking congregations.

It closed in the 1980s. Eventually, it was upgraded for the Edinburgh Festival and other events. The Sculpture Stair features 320 figures representing 50 years of the festival. The adaptive reuse in 1999 was and is instructive. The Old Town is not a museum; heritage preservation can be as much about the future as it is of the past.

57

The Ensign Ewart

521-523 Lawnmarket

A tavern since 1680 and one of the few to retain a name from the Napoleonic Wars, a custom once common. Charles Ewart of the Royal North British Dragoons (Scots Greys) famously seized the standard of a French unit at the Battle of Waterloo. The standard (a gilded bronze eagle) is in the regiment's museum at Edinburgh Castle; a painting, *The Fight For The Standard*, is in the Great Hall. The ensign's granite memorial is on Castle Esplanade.

58

Patrick Geddes Centre

Riddle's Court, 322 Lawnmarket

1590; later additions; Stewart Henbest Capper & George Shaw Aitken
1888–95; LDN Architects, Elliott & Company engineers 2017

The court is through a close in a 1720s tenement built by George Riddle, a wright and burgess. At the entrance on the Lawnmarket are Riddle's name and the date 1888–95, from renovation, led by conservationist and sociologist Patrick Geddes, as halls of residence for the University of Edinburgh.

Geddes advocated an organic patchwork of urban renewal, keeping existing fabric where practical (buildings judged beyond repair in the court here were demolished and an outside staircase fitted to link two exposed levels). Much of the Old Town's heritage that survived slum clearance and has been restored is due to his work and influence. His motto 'Vivendo Discimus', meaning 'by living we learn' is carved above an arch in the courtyard.

Originally, this was the townhouse of Bailie MacMorran, a merchant with royal connections who, in 1595, was shot dead by a student while enforcing the law at High School Yards. His house was so well-appointed that, in 1598, the town council chose it for a banquet for James VI, his queen and visiting Danish nobles. In 1751, David Hume (see 64) rented rooms here.

In the 20th century, Riddle's Court was an adult learning centre and Edinburgh Festival venue. Scottish Historic Buildings Trust leased it in 2011 for rehabilitation as the Patrick Geddes Centre, which opened in 2017. It is an accretion of historic features restored as a narrative, not frozen to a fixed period in time. Modern interventions are discreet and stylish.

59

Gladstone's Land

477b Lawnmarket

c. 1550

The archaic 'land' in Scots means a tenement or apartment house. This is one of the oldest on the Royal Mile. In 1934, it became the first property bought

by the newly formed National Trust for Scotland. Painted walls and ceilings (c. 1620) were uncovered during restoration. A turnpike stair (everything had to be carried up this way, including water) serves the six-storey structure. The golden bird clutching a rat above the entrance is a glede (red kite). It refers to a 17th-century owner, merchant Thomas Gledstanes, who extended the building out front on a ground floor arcade, a feature once common in Edinburgh and other Scottish towns. He lived above it and rented the rest of the property, a social strata typical of the Old Town at the time.

The Saltire Society, founded in 1936 to promote Scottish culture, was once based here. Its credo was 'The nation that forgets its past is dead.' The society is very much alive, at 9 Fountain Close, 22 High Street.

60

Lady Stair's House
Lady Stair's Close, Lawnmarket
1622; George Shaw Aitken 1897
Named for the Countess of Stair, a descendant of the original owners, merchant William Gray and his wife Geida Smith. Their initials are carved on the door lintel; also the date and a typical 'sermon in stone' – 'Fear the Lord and depart from Evil.'

The Scots Baronial tower dates from restoration/reconstruction initiated by Patrick Geddes for the 5th Earl of Rosebery, who was descended from the original owners. In 1907, the earl gave the building to the city as a history museum, now The Writers' Museum dedicated to Burns, Scott and Stevenson. Inside, there is a compelling collection of memorabilia associated with them. Outside is Makars' (Poets') Court with paving inscribed with Scottish writers' quotes selected by the Saltire Society.

61

Deacon Brodie's Tavern
435 Lawnmarket
18th century; Peter Henderson (tavern) 1894

Tenement with a ground floor bar named after Deacon Brodie, 'respected citizen by day, burglar at night', who went to trial in 1788, was found guilty and hanged. He had been a cabinetmaker, Deacon of the Incorporation of Wrights and Masons and a town councillor. His double life is often cited as the source of Robert Louis Stevenson's novel *The Strange Case of Dr Jekyll and Mr Hyde*. Across the street is Brodie's Close where his family home was.

62

Bank of Scotland Headquarters
The Mound (North Bank Street)

Richard Crichton & Robert Reid c. 1802–6; David Bryce 1864–70

The Bank of Scotland, founded in 1695, is the oldest Scottish bank. It strides into the Old Town from the top of The Mound, where the dome above the entrance says 'look at me'.

What you see today rises from a massive podium and retaining wall on Market Street, on which stood the bank's building of 1806. Architect David Bryce's flamboyant Victorian reconstruction gave the bank tremendous visual presence. The dome, topped with a statue of Fame, dominates the view here, but the baroque panoply of pediments, classical columns and caryatids is best seen from Princes Street (photo on page 84). Statues (John Rhind sculptor) symbolise Britannia and her Children; also History and Geography, Navigation and Commerce, Prosperity and Plenty.

On the south-facing piano nobile is the bank's coat of arms with figures of Abundance and Justice (John Marshall & Samuel Mackenzie sculptors 1809) salvaged from the original building. The timber-framed, copper-clad dome, found to be close to collapse in the early 1990s, was rebuilt, steel-framed and reclad by the bank's in-house architects, and Fame regilded for the tricentennial. The Bryce Hall, subdivided for offices, was restored to its double-height splendour during refurbishment (Malcolm Fraser Architects

2006). The hall overlooks Princes Street and the New Town. The governor and directors could gaze out from here and feel they ruled the world. The history of the bank is told in the Museum on the Mound (part of the refurbishment); entrance downhill on North Bank Street.

63

Institut Français Écosse
George IV Bridge

'A little corner of France in the heart of Edinburgh', originally Midlothian County Buildings, later Lothian Chambers (James Macintyre Henry & Thomas Forbes Maclennan 1904). It faces George IV Bridge (the façade shown here) and West Parliament Square. Classical figures (William Birnie Rhind sculptor) represented the county's economy – agriculture, fishing and coal mining.

The interior, evocative of Edwardian civic self-confidence, was refurbished in 2017 for the French Consulate and the French Institute in Scotland. Their presence in Edinburgh's old royal, religious and parliamentary quarter recalls the Auld Alliance, the royal, military and cultural bond that lasted from the Franco-Scottish treaty of 1295 until the Reformation. The institute hosts visual arts and music; there is a library, language school, diplomatic offices and, naturally, a bistro.

64

David Hume statue
High Street

Alexander Stoddart sculptor 1997
'Philosopher and Historian, Scot and European. Man of the Enlightenment' are inscribed on the back of the plinth on which the hero of the Scottish Enlightenment sits dressed like an ancient philosopher. The tribute was commissioned by the Saltire Society to mark its 60th anniversary. Nearby, in front of St Giles' High Kirk, is the 5th Duke of Buccleuch (Joseph Edgar Boehm sculptor 1888). The panels on its pedestal illustrate historic events and the duke's life and times. Passersby don't much bother with him but have taken to rubbing Hume's big toe, perhaps for wisdom or good luck.

65

St Giles' High Kirk

High Street

1385–1410; William Burn 1829–33; William Hay 1871–9, & Henderson 1881–4

St Giles' stands like an island of stone pinnacles on the Royal Mile, the result

of 'improvements' in the early 19th-century which removed the Old Tolbooth (c. 1400) and a row of shops – the Luckenbooths (traders' lockable booths) – in a row of tenements a handshake away (cobblestones show where they and the Tolbooth were). The city's medieval heritage was further eroded around 1830 when the kirk was reclad in Gothic Revival style by architect William Burn. Observing the alterations some decades later, Robert Louis Stevenson condemned 'zealous magistrates and a misguided architect' and said the church 'if it were not for the spire, would be unrecognisable'.

The original 12th-century kirk was built in Norman (Romanesque) style. It was looted and burned during the invasion of Scotland in 1385 by Richard II. It was reconstructed and enlarged over the following centuries. Its 15th-century crown steeple (the spire), repaired in 1648 (John Mylne master mason), is one of three from the Middle Ages to survive in Scotland (the others are in Aberdeen and Glasgow). Carved stone heads on its obelisk symbolise the four winds of heaven. The tower is supported on four massive internal pillars.

After the Reformation, the kirk was stripped of Catholic symbols and subdivided for separate congregations. Charles I in 1633, the year of his Scottish coronation, proclaimed the kirk a cathedral, a designation that lingers. In 1871, Lord Provost William Chambers sponsored reinstatement of the pre-Reformation volume to reveal, for the first time in three centuries, the perspective, some 60 metres from the west door to the east window. The west front was rebuilt and embellished with sculptures (John Rhind 1884) of Scottish monarchs, clerics and Saint Giles.

Inside, is a host of historic characters: a statue of John Knox, the kirk's preacher of the Reformation (James Pittendrigh Macgillivray sculptor 1906), effigies of the Marquess of Montrose and Marquess of Argyll, enemies during the civil wars of the 17th century, and Robert Louis Stevenson (Augustus Saint-Gaudens sculptor 1904); also memorials to ministers and the military. Edinburgh's trade guilds are represented by their respective saints on the screen to the north transept. The transept is illuminated by the Great North Window, 'Christ Stilling the Tempest' (Douglas Strachan artist 1922).

A renewal programme (Simpson & Brown Architects 1979–90) prioritised restoration and conservation while responding to changing patterns of worship and tourism. The primary purpose was to place the communion table at the centre under the crossing (it was at the east end before), and surround it with an inner ring for worship and an outer ring for visitors. A striking feature is the Burns Memorial Window (Leifur Breidfjord artist 1985) above the west door, which replaced a Victorian window that could not be repaired.

66
The Thistle Chapel
St Giles' High Kirk

Robert Lorimer 1910
Scotland's ancient order of chivalry, the Order of the Thistle, was revived in 1687 by James VII who created a chapel at Holyrood Abbey for its

knights. They lost it when the king was deposed in 1688. The order was dormant until 1703, and without a chapel until this one was purpose built, snug against the great kirk of St Giles' (the preferred site was the abbey ruin, but it would not support a new roof).

The style is 15th-century Gothic, with an exceptional Arts and Crafts decorative scheme crowned with a fan-vaulted ceiling and packed with ornament, like jewels in a box. Shining among them are carved ceiling bosses, heraldic emblems and angels, some playing bagpipes. There is a throne for the sovereign and stalls for the knights. Architect Lorimer went on to win the competition for the Scottish National War Memorial (see 52).

67
Signet Library
Parliament Square
William Stark 1812–22

George IV in 1822 declared this 'the finest drawing room in Europe'. It was the Advocates Library until acquired by The Society of Writers to the Signet (writers of documents sealed with the Signet, the personal seal of Scottish monarchs). The advocates commissioned a new library (William Playfair 1833). Both are part of the old Scottish Parliament complex, which houses the Supreme Courts of Scotland. The Signet Library has two opulent neoclassical rooms. The lower room later became a tearoom. The upper one, which impressed George IV, is a vaulted promenade lined with Corinthian columns. Halfway along is a dome with painted figures of Apollo and the Muses, poets, philosophers and historians. A stained glass window (1887) commemorates the Golden Jubilee of Queen Victoria.

68
Old Parliament Hall
Old Parliament House, Parliament Square
James Murray 'Principal Master of all His Majesties works in Scotland' & John Scott master wright 1632–40

Behind a ponderous neoclassical façade is this magnificent hall, the first purpose built debating chamber for the Scottish Parliament and the oldest of its type in the British Isles. The hall, with an oak trussed roof and an undercroft, is virtually all that is left of the original 17th-century building.

Old Parliament House was Edinburgh's finest civic building, ordered built by Charles I to house the Parliament, Privy Council and Court of Session. The Jacobean-style exterior sprouted bartizans and turrets, and had a

Renaissance-style doorway bearing royal insignia and statues of Mercy and Justice. The statues (Alexander Mylne sculptor 1636) were removed around 1805, when the bulk of the building was demolished to enlarge the Supreme Courts on Parliament Square (Robert Reid architect). They were thought lost until spotted in an antiquarian's garden in the New Town and returned for display. The loss of the Jacobean architecture, a symbol of the independence of Scotland, was lamented. Reid's neoclassicism was condemned. Henry Cockburn wrote, 'No one who remembers the old exterior can see the new one without sorrow and indignation.'

After the Act of Union of 1707, the hall was used by the courts and for public functions. Displayed are portraits and sculptures of notable persons. The stained glass South Window (1868) shows James V in 1532 establishing

the Court of Session (the supreme civil court), the foundation of Scotland's legal system. Outside is Charles II cast in lead, riding forth like a Roman emperor. The statue (1685), attributed to Dutch sculptor Grinling Gibbons, is the city's oldest. A tribute (in Latin) is inscribed 'To Charles the Second, most august and most magnificent, the invincible ruler of Britain, France and Ireland, upon whose birth Divine Providence smiled . . .'

69
Mercat Cross
Parliament Square
Sidney Mitchell 1885; restored 2018
A replica of the Mercat (market) Cross erected in 1617, where royal and civic proclamations were made and merchants met. In 1756, it was declared an obstruction to traffic and 'utterly destroyed by a misguided hand'. So wrote William Ewart Gladstone who paid for its reincarnation. The unicorn, carved by John Rhind in 1869, is a traditional symbol of Scottish royalty; the shaft on which it sits is a reproduction erected in 1970. The capital, carved with dragons and foliage, is believed to have been recycled in 1617 from an earlier cross.

In 1750, a visitor stood here and said (of the Scottish Enlightenment) he could 'in a few minutes, take 50 men of genius and learning by the hand'. Among the men of genius were David Hume and Adam Smith. A statue of Smith is here (Alexander Stoddart sculptor 2008); Hume too, nearby (see 64); also the figure (Kenny Mackay sculptor 2008) of James Braidwood (see 161).

70
City Chambers (former Royal Exchange)
253 High Street
John & Robert Adam 1753–61

In 1811, the town council moved from the Old Tolbooth to the Royal Exchange. The historic but decrepit Tolbooth was demolished in 1817. The Exchange was not intended for the town council. It was the first of Lord Provost George Drummond's 'city improvement' projects, a commercial building with a customs house as the centrepiece and a piazza for merchants to meet and trade. To the project's disadvantage, the merchants continued to meet at the Mercat Cross. When the lease of the Customs House expired, the Exchange was repurposed as the City Chambers.

Edinburgh grew in the 19th century and the City Chambers with it. An annex (Robert Morham City Architect 1898–1904) was built on Cockburn Street and an arcaded screen with the city's coat of arms (William Birnie Rhind sculptor 1903) on the Royal Mile. In the courtyard is the dramatic 'Alexander and Bucephalus' (John Steell sculptor). The design, first exhibited in 1833, was cast in bronze fifty years later. It shows the horse spooked by its shadow, and Alexander the Great turning it towards the sun to tame it. The statue, unveiled on St Andrew Square in 1884, was relocated here in 1916 to make way for Gladstone (see 126).

Entombed under the City Chambers is Mary King's Close, 'Edinburgh's deepest secret'. A macabre myth lingers that the close was quarantined during the plague of 1645 and victims inside were left to their fate. Later residents reported paranormal activity. This was a boon when the close was reopened for tours in 2003, ghosts included.

The spirit of place

'Many people are drawn to Calton Hill as a special place for our nation. On a fine, breezy day here you can think clearly and see far. It is extraordinary that in the centre of Edinburgh there should be a place which feels like it connects directly to the whole country beyond the city that surrounds it.'

—*Malcolm Fraser, architect*

The view from Calton Hill has been the definitive image of Edinburgh since 1690 when Captain John Slezer, a military surveyor, drew it. It was reproduced in *Theatrum Scotiae*, an album of his engravings of Scottish castles, palaces and towns. The photograph above shows the monument (1831) to philosopher Dugald Stewart. The design, inspired by the Athenian Choragic Monument of Lysicrates, was by William Playfair, architect of 'The Athens of the North'. Calton Hill was acquired by the town council in 1724 to create Edinburgh's first public park.

2

Calton Hill, Princes Street
& the New Town

*National Monument of Scotland—Collective Gallery—Royal High
School—St Andrew's House—Old Calton Burying Ground—Balmoral
Hotel—Café Royal—RW Forsyth Building—St Andrew Square—
Scottish National Portrait Gallery—Mansfield Traquair Centre—
St Andrew's Church—Jenners Department Store Building—Scott
Monument—The Mound—Robert Louis Stevenson House—Charlotte
Square—Moray Place...*

71

National Monument of Scotland

Calton Hill

Charles Robert Cockerell & William Playfair 1822–29

The Earl of Elgin laid the 6-ton foundation stone for this memorial to Scots in the British armed forces who died in the Napoleonic Wars. The ceremony was accompanied by cannon salutes from Edinburgh Castle and Salisbury Crags. King George IV was patron of the project.

The organising committee of 'Noblemen and Gentlemen of Scotland' considered several designs, among them an enormous classical rotunda (Archibald Elliot architect) modelled on the Pantheon in Rome, proposed for The Mound. Calton Hill was preferred, and Greek Revival style. Architect and archaeologist Charles Cockerell, who had visited Athens and made drawings of the Parthenon, was appointed on Elgin's advice. Elgin also knew the Parthenon, having acquired much of its ornament (the 'Elgin Marbles', displayed in the British Museum, London). William Playfair was the executive architect. Funds were sought by public subscription.

The mission was epic. Teams of horses hauled huge blocks of sandstone from Craigleith Quarry to the top of Calton Hill. A great hall was planned, to have been a temple or pantheon, wrapped with 46 Greek Doric columns and crowned at each end with a prodigious pediment. Twelve columns and an architrave were erected before fund raising faltered and the project was abandoned. It was derided as 'Edinburgh's disgrace', but the 'failed

Parthenon' on the acropolis that is Calton Hill remains the symbol of the 'Athens of the North'.

Less prominent but more significant today than the failed Parthenon is the Democracy Cairn (1998). It commemorates the five-year vigil kept on Regent Road during the campaign for a Scottish parliament (see 3). Built by the keepers of the vigil.

72

Nelson Monument
Calton Hill

Robert Burn 1807

Annually on Trafalgar Day, flags are flown from this telescope-shaped tower erected to commemorate Nelson's famous victory. A zinc-clad wooden 'time ball' on a mast was fitted in 1853 by Charles Piazzi Smyth, Astronomer Royal. The ball could be seen by mariners at Leith who

when it was raised and dropped at 1.00 pm set their chronometers, except when sea fog rolled in. Sound was provided in 1861 by the One o'Clock Gun at the castle. The correct time, recorded at the Royal Observatory, was transmitted from the monument to the castle by cable, the longest wire in the world at the time. The monument's castellated style was chosen to complement Robert Adam's Calton Jail (see 77).

73

City Observatory (Collective Gallery)
Calton Hill

William Playfair 1818

A temple of celestial enquiry, a perfect symbol of the Scottish Enlightenment and of the 'Athens of the North'. It is said to have been inspired in spirit by the Tower of the Winds, an ancient Athenian weather station. Edinburgh's observatory, with its Greek cross plan, Roman Doric porches on all four sides and a central dome, is the purest of William Playfair's works. He was

influenced by neoclassical architect William Stark, under whom he trained. Intriguingly, Stark produced 'beautiful designs for an observatory on Calton Hill' for the Earl of Elgin, but no drawings are known to survive.

Playfair's building is the centrepiece in a walled compound completed by him in 1824. On its south-east corner is the Playfair Monument (1822) honouring not the architect but his uncle John Playfair, President of the Astronomical Institution which commissioned the observatory. On the south-west corner, in castellated Gothic style suggested by Robert Adam, is Old Observatory House (James Craig 1776) where lived Thomas Short, brother of telescope-maker James Short who planned an observatory here. The Scots Baronial extension (1883) was constructed for Astronomer Royal, Charles Piazzi Smyth.

The Short brothers' observatory, a classical domed octagon by Craig, thought not to have been completed, was replaced by Playfair's temple (renamed the Royal Observatory in 1822). When the Royal Observatory relocated to Blackford Hill (see 189) the site reverted to the city. The City Dome (Robert Morham, City Architect 1895) was built on the compound's northeast corner for a telescope too large to fit Playfair's building. The Astronomical Society of Edinburgh occupied the site from 1924 until 2008, when the buildings were abandoned and left to decay. In 2014, Malcolm Fraser Architects won a competition and devised a plan for their adaptive reuse. The clients were contemporary art group Collective and the city, which owns the site. The project was completed with sensitivity and restraint by Collective Architecture. Collective Gallery opened in 2018.

The historic site has been transformed into one of the most unexpected and exciting venues for art in Scotland. The ground is landscaped as a 'constellation' of wildflowers and plants (HarrisonStevens landscape design). A restaurant, The Lookout, its architecture clearly new, is cantilevered above the city on the previously vacant northwest corner (Elliot & Company engineers). The ground on the north side of Playfair's observatory was excavated for The Hillside exhibition and office space with a rooftop viewing deck. Conservation of Playfair's observatory (still with telescope) was aided by the architect's original drawings. Artworks, food and a 19th-century telescope? Brilliant. Thrilling views too. RIAS Award 2019 and RIBA Award for Scotland 2019.

74
Royal High School
Regent Road
Thomas Hamilton 1825–9
It is generally accepted that the Royal High was established in 1128, as the seminary at Holyrood Abbey. After the Reformation, Mary Queen of Scots in 1566 transferred it to the town council. It is still a public (not private) school, one of the oldest in Europe. It was located at High School Yards (see 32) before moving to Calton Hill when the eastern New Town was developed. In 1968, the school relocated to the suburbs. Since then, its outstanding Greek Revival building hugging the south side of Calton Hill has been empty.

Its hall was refurbished in 1979 for a Scottish Assembly that never assembled. It was considered and dismissed as a home for the new Scottish Parliament or a national museum of photography, being near Rock House (see 78). Controversial plans to turn it into a luxury hotel were rejected by the Scottish Government after a public inquiry in 2020. The Royal High School Preservation Trust proposes the building be repurposed for St Mary's Music School.

75

Burns Monument
Regent Road
Thomas Hamilton c. 1834
Memorial to the 'heaven-taught ploughman', as Edinburgh socialites described Robert Burns, elevated here in architecture inspired by ancient Greece. The Dugald Stewart Monument (page 58) is of similar design, as is the Burns Monument (Thomas Hamilton 1820) at Alloway, Ayrshire, the bard's birthplace. A statue of him originally inside this rotunda is in the National Portrait Gallery (see 91).

76

St Andrew's House
Regent Road
Thomas Tait 1934–9; refurbished Reiach & Hall Architects 2002 for the Scottish Government
Awesome Art Deco block for the Scottish Office, the British state's agency in Scotland. It was commissioned from Burnet, Tait & Lorne, a London-Scottish practice, after a banal design of 1929 by HM Office of Works in London outraged the Scottish cultural establishment. Even the Palace commented: 'Their Majesties take a great interest in the City of Edinburgh, and they do hope that something noble and worthy of this site may be built.' Accordingly, the architects, principally Thomas Tait, made St Andrew's House fit the landscape, as Thomas Hamilton did with the Royal High School.

The decorative programme was assertively Scottish. The pillars flanking the entrance are decorated with thistles. The bas-relief on the bronze doors (Walter Gilbert sculptor) is a mystical tableau with Saint Andrew by the Sea of Galilee being called to follow Jesus (symbolising the mission of public service). The travertine floor in the foyer has the Saltire embedded. Walnut

panelling in the former office of the Secretary of State is said to have come from a tree planted by Mary Queen of Scots.

Above the entrance is the nation's royal heraldry (Alexander Carrick sculptor) and, flanking six pilasters, heraldic relief panels (Phyllis Bone). Figures on the pilasters represent Architecture, Statecraft, Health, Agriculture, Fisheries and Education (William Reid Dick & Alexander Carrick). St Andrew's House was the largest steel-framed building in Europe at the time. The centre block's 'step-back' massing was fashionably north American; at each end of its wings is a Bauhaus-style stair tower, a modernist conceit in the historic setting.

77
Calton Jail Governor's House
Regent Road
Archibald Elliot 1817
Governor's House (seen here from the Old Town) was part of Calton Jail (Robert Adam 1792–6), once the biggest prison in Scotland. It was a forbidding Gothic fortress on the side of Calton Hill. Tourists arriving by

train below the hill sometimes mistook it for Edinburgh Castle. When the jail was demolished, to make way for St Andrew's House, Governor's House was spared and refurbished as part of the Scottish Office complex.

78

Rock House

28 Calton Hill Street

Below the monuments on Calton Hill is this landmark in the history of photography – the home of Robert Adamson, who formed a partnership with David Octavius Hill in 1843. Their photographic studio was here; their focus Edinburgh, its places and people (their work can be seen in the National Portrait Gallery).

The house (1765) is at the end of a block of 18th-century tenements once part of the Barony of Calton, which was incorporated into Edinburgh in 1856. At the end of the street is the former Calton Convening Rooms (Archibald Elliot 1818) where the Incorporated Trades of Calton met. The building replaced their old hall which was demolished when Waterloo Place and Regent Bridge were constructed to access the eastern New Town.

79

Old Calton Burying Ground

Waterloo Place

The cemetery was established by the Incorporated Trades of Calton in 1718. A century later, it was bisected when Waterloo Place was constructed.

The north section (gate on Calton Hill Street) has the oldest gravestone, erected in 1720 for a shoemaker. Monuments in the south section reflect wealth and privilege. Ironically, they are dominated by The Political Martyrs' Monument (Thomas Hamilton 1844). The obelisk was 'Erected by the Friends of Parliamentary Reform' to the memory of five radicals who were charged

in 1793 of sedition and sentenced to be transported to Botany Bay, the penal colony in Australia. At the time, most people did not have the right to vote. The British elite, fearing contagion from the French Revolution, ruthlessly suppressed the radical movement. The monument was dedicated before a crowd of 3,000 people.

The finest piece of architecture here is the tomb of David Hume (Robert Adam 1778), a cylindrical Roman mausoleum at once muscular and refined. Next to Hume is Abraham Lincoln acknowledged by a freed slave – a memorial to Scottish-Americans who fought against the slave-owing Confederates in the American Civil War (George Edwin Bissell sculptor 1893).

80

Balmoral Hotel

1 Princes Street

William Hamilton Beattie (George Beattie & Son) 1896-1902

Originally the North British Hotel, the second largest railway hotel in Britain after St Pancras in London. A competition for it was held in 1895. The winner, W H Beattie, accompanied the general manager and directors of the North British Railway Company on a recce of hotels on the Continent before finalising the design, a pick-and-mix from his grand tour. He died in 1898; his assistant, Andrew Robb Scott, completed the project.

The clock tower has been a landmark at the east end of Princes Street since 1902 – the clock set fast so travellers won't miss their trains (three minutes fast, except on Hogmanay). In 1991, the hotel was refurbished and rebranded The Balmoral (a reference to Queen Victoria's castle in the Highlands). It overlooks Waverley Station, constructed in several stages (1846–1902). The name was inspired by the popularity of Walter Scott's *Waverley* novels. The station's steel and glass roof, supported on cast iron Corinthian columns, was reglazed during refurbishment by Network Rail (2009–14). At concourse level is the original Renaissance-style Booking Hall (c. 1900).

81

National Records of Scotland, General Register House
2 Princes Street
Robert & James Adam 1774–88

Register House is the first purpose built archives and public record office in Britain and one of the oldest in the world still used as designed.

A public building on this site was anticipated by James Craig (noted on his revised New

Town Plan of 1768). As intended, it is best seen from North Bridge, from where Robert Adam's Palladian façade (part of it) and dome are striking. The complete elevation is obscured by the later North British Hotel (previous entry) and the former Post Office building.

The foundation stone for Register House was laid in 1774. In 1779, work stopped for six years until funding, originally from forfeited Jacobite estates, resumed. Brick storage vaults and stone floors were specified to resist damp and fire. The domed rotunda was inspired by the Pantheon in Rome. Its ceiling is decorated with delicate plasterwork (Thomas Clayton junior) typical of Adam's style, the classical theme here infiltrated with Scottish thistles. The space was renovated in 2008 for the 'ScotlandsPeople Centre' where family histories can be traced.

In front of Register House is an energetic equestrian bronze statue of the Duke of Wellington (John Steell sculptor 1852). At the back is the north section of the archives (Robert Reid 1822–7), a second rotunda and New Register House (Robert Matheson 1859–63); also the Archivists' Garden (Gross. Max. landscape design 2010) with species relating to Scotland's past and people.

82

Cowan's Warehouse

West Register Street Lane

> *William Hamilton Beattie (George Beattie &*
> *Son) 1864*

Venetian Gothic fantasy, originally the printing and stationery warehouse of Alex Cowan & Sons. Its ogee-arched windows and carvings of reptiles, animals, birds and plants look like an illustration from Ruskin's *The Stones of Venice*, probably an influence. Alex Cowan was a friend of Walter Scott, who wrote on Cowan-made paper; editions of the *Waverley* novels were printed on it. The building is part of The Registers, a mixed-use development (Hoskins Architects, Will Rudd Davidson engineers 2019). The historic timber and cast iron structure was demolished but the façade was restored and secured to new construction, a steel-framed office block, and the mansard roof recreated.

83

Café Royal

19 West Register

Street

> *Robert Paterson*
> *1863; James*
> *Macintyre Henry*
> *(interior) c. 1900*

Parisian-style corner block with a bar on

the ground floor famed for its Royal Doulton ceramic tile panels depicting famous inventors; also stained glass (James Ballantine studio) painted with sporting scenes (archery, deer stalking, lawn bowling, tennis, fox hunting and fishing). The tiled panels were promotional exhibits for Doulton at the International Inventions Exhibition of 1885 in London. They were displayed in Edinburgh the following year, at the International Exhibition of Industry, Science and Art; and later installed in the Café Royal Hotel and Oyster Bar, as it was called at the time. The seafood theme is advertised with a model of a lobster on the wrought iron sign outside.

84
R W Forsyth Building
30 Princes Street

John James Burnet architect,
Redpath, Brown & Co. engineers
1907

Former department store of 'Ladies and Gents Outfitter' Robert Wallace Forsyth, for whom J J Burnet had built a Parisian-style emporium in Glasgow. Burnet visited North America in 1896 and returned with enthusiasm for steel-frame construction and the challenge of how to persuade his conservative clients to accept the new technology. 'Hide it' was the answer. Forsyth's is stone-clad, embellished with Ionic columns and sculpture (William Birnie Rhind & William Reid Dick), but with the internal grid of steel expressed on rectilinear façades. It is thought to be the first fully steel-framed building in Scotland. The store closed in 1981. On the tower is the much-loved Forsyth Globe decorated with *putti* and signs of the zodiac.

85
R W Forsyth Annex
3 St Andrew Square

John James Burnet 1925

Baroque façade with an Italianate eaves gallery, tall and narrow like Burnet's work in Edwardian Glasgow. Retrofitted as luxury flats, it is part of a commercial development, 3–8 St Andrew Square (CDA Group & Hoskins Architects 2016), for which two Victorian relics and the 20th-century heritage-listed Scottish Provident Building (Rowand Anderson, Kininmonth & Paul 1969) were demolished, the latter controversially in 2014.

86
British Linen Bank
38 St Andrew Square

David Bryce c. 1850

Palladian design derived from the Loggia del Capitaniato, Vicenza. Statues

represent Navigation, Commerce, Manufacturing, Architecture, Industry and Agriculture (Alexander Handyside Ritchie sculptor). Fabulous interior with a classical domed banking hall. In 2018, planning permission was given for adaptive reuse (3DReid Architects, Simpson & Brown conservation architects) as Gleneagles Club hotel.

The British Linen Company was founded in the Old Town in 1746 to finance the Scottish linen industry. The 'British' tag reflected the reality of Hanoverian supremacy after the Jacobite rising of 1745 was crushed at Culloden. Street names in the New Town also conformed to the new reality: most were named to please George III (St Andrew Square and Thistle Street are exceptions). But for this deference, Princes Street would have been St Giles Street, after the city's patron saint. Instead, it flattered the king's eldest son, the future George IV.

87

Prudential Assurance Building

1–2 St Andrew Square

Alfred Waterhouse & Son 1895

Above the door on the turreted corner tower is a statue of Prudence (William Birnie Rhind sculptor), the public face of the Prudential, founded in London in 1848. Many branches were built in Northern Renaissance style. Most were designed by Alfred Waterhouse and clad in terracotta and red brick, a Victorian example of corporate branding. This was rejected in Edinburgh in favour of stone, thought more in keeping with the city's historic urban texture (stone cladding remains the default choice of city planners). In the 1990s, the interior was replaced. The Victorian ceramic tile-clad former business hall was retained, repurposed as Tiles café/bar.

88

Melville Monument

St Andrew Square

William Burn architect, Robert Stevenson engineer, Francis Chantrey & Robert Forrest sculptors 1821–3; Gillespies landscape design 2008

St Andrew Square is dominated by this colossal classical column on which stands Henry Dundas, 1st Viscount Melville who ruled Scotland for the British state in the late 18th century. No political appointment could be made without his patronage. He represented an unelected elite opposed to democracy. In 1792, protesters burned his effigy during three days of riots in Edinburgh. He was responsible for the exile of radicals – among them, those commemorated on the obelisk in Old Calton Burying Ground (see 79).

He promoted imperialism in South Africa and India. A cartoon of 1788 by James Gilray in the National Portrait Gallery collection shows him as part kilted Scot, part turbaned Bengal despot. In 1806, he was impeached on the charge of misappropriation of public money while First Lord of the Admiralty, acquitted, but never again held public office. The most damning charge against him is that in 1792, to protect economic interests, he delayed the abolition of the slave trade in British colonies for 15 years, causing the transportation to the West Indies and enslavement of about 630,000 Africans.

The monument was funded by navy personnel. Lighthouse engineer Robert Stevenson was hired to allay fears the column would fall down. It deserves to stay but Melville should be deposed. Of all the figures in Edinburgh's public places, he is the least deserving of the honour. In 2008, when privately owned St Andrew Square was leased to the city for public access, the monument's disturbing symbolism was not acknowledged, such was the cloud of amnesia that hid the truth about Scots and slavery. In 2020, following the Black Lives Matter protests, text for a long-overdue plaque exposing Melville's activities was agreed.

89

Dundas House

36 St Andrew Square

William Chambers 1771–4

Palladian villa built for Laurence Dundas, cousin of Henry Dundas. He gained wealth and status as a contractor to the Duke of Cumberland during the Jacobite rising of 1745. James Boswell described him 'a cunning shrewd man of the world'. His shrewdest move, having seen James Craig's New Town Plan, was to secure this site next to land he owned. Craig intended a church here (see 96).

In 1795, the villa became the Excise Office (hence the royal coat of arms on the pediment). In 1825, it was bought by the Royal Bank of Scotland. The Adamesque dining room became the bank's boardroom. The drawing room was removed to create a double-height foyer (William Burn 1836). A plaque here marks the spot from where the New Town Plan was measured.

The statue outside is of Peninsular War hero, politician and governor of the bank, the 4th Earl of Hopetoun dressed as a Roman imperial consul (Thomas Campbell sculptor 1834; inscription by Walter Scott). In 2020, RBS announced a review to consider the statue's future – the earl was involved in suppressing a slave revolt in Grenada and had a family link with Laurence Dundas, who owned plantations in the West Indies.

90

Royal Bank of Scotland Banking Hall

36 St Andrew Square

John Dick Peddie 1857; Michael Laird Architects, Graven design 2015

Magnificent Roman-style banking hall attached to the rear of Dundas House. Its iron dome is studded with 120 coffered stars. The spandrels contain medallions animated with playful *putti* symbolising Agriculture, Arts, Navigation and Trade. The hall still serves the bank's customers. Recent conservation and refurbishment revealed that the original floor was paved with Minton tiles. Some are now visible, displayed under a panel of toughened glass.

91
Scottish National Portrait Gallery
1 Queen Street

> *Robert Rowand Anderson 1885–90; Page\Park Architects, Will Rudd Davidson engineers 2011*

A pantheon of Scotland's elite and its achievements

sponsored by John Ritchie Findlay, philanthropist and publisher of *The Scotsman*. Style, Venetian Gothic, modelled on the Doge's Palace. Allegorical and historical figures on the façade (William Birnie Rhind sculptor, et al., 1890–1906) represent the Arts, Science, History, Religion, Industry and famous Scots, among them Wallace and Bruce who guard the entrance. On the roofline is Clio, muse of History in Greek mythology (Alexander Stoddart sculptor 2013); it replaced Birnie Rhind's figure which was eroded beyond repair. In the Great Hall is a marble statue of Robert Burns by John Flaxman (see 75) and a portrait memorial to benefactor Findlay. The highlight is a glittering frieze of characters from Scotland's past (William Brassey Hole artist).

Page\Park restored the much-altered Victorian interiors, revealed the structure's original riveted steel I-beams, rationalised access to all three floors and improved lighting and energy efficiency. Formerly dull salons are now bright. Interventions, like the glass elevator, are crisp and contemporary. There is more display space than before, notably for curatorial initiatives that include socially inclusive contemporary art and photography. Interpretative panels throughout are informed by 21st-century scholarship. Originally the building was shared with the National Museum of Antiquities; a relic of that period, the Society of Antiquaries Library, has been reinstated. The gallery has many portraits by Henry Raeburn. Some were painted in his studio at Raeburn House (1798), nearby at 32 York Place (inscription on a plaque shaped like an artist's palette on the façade).

92

Mansfield Traquair Centre

15 Mansfield Place

Robert Rowand Anderson 1873–85;

Phoebe Traquair artist 1893–1901

Nothing outside this Romanesque Revival former church prepares you for its extraordinary interior – 'Edinburgh's Sistine Chapel', a barrel-vaulted nave, chancel and side chapels covered with murals. The work was commissioned by the Catholic Apostolic Church whose members believed in the Second Coming of Christ. The interior was decorated accordingly by Arts and Crafts artist Phoebe Traquair (the Second Coming is imagined, painted on the west wall). The effect is of illuminated manuscripts come to life, magnified and reinterpreted in early Renaissance and Pre-Raphaelite styles.

The congregation moved out in 1958. In 1992, the Friends of Mansfield Place Church (as it was called) started a campaign to save the building from decay. It was bought in 1998 by the Mansfield Traquair Trust and was born again as The Mansfield Traquair Centre, an events venue. Offices for the Scottish Council for Voluntary Organisations were created in the undercroft (Simpson & Brown Architects 2000–2). A two-year restoration of the paintings, led by Historic (now Historic Environment) Scotland's Conservation Centre, was completed in 2005.

Phoebe Traquair painted other murals in Edinburgh: at St Mary's Cathedral Song School (see 130) and the Royal Hospital for Sick Children (201). A what-might-have-been is that in 1892 she turned down the chance to decorate the Great Hall at the National Portrait Gallery.

93
Richard Murphy House
2b Hart Street
Richard Murphy 2014

The architect started out doing mews conversions, none as playful and personal as his house here. City council approved it after planners recommended refusal. Of Edinburgh, Murphy once wrote, 'This is a city where many citizens wish that the modern era had never occurred. Modern architecture, it seems to be universally agreed, has spoilt the view.'

On Hart Street, at the eastern edge of the New Town, there wasn't much of a view to spoil. The house is steel-framed, partly stone-clad in keeping with the urban context. Inside, it is a 'vertical cabinet of curiosities' with living spaces created ingeniously out of the tight site. Eco-friendly too, with a ground source heat pump, rainwater harvesting and a south-facing glass roof angled for solar panels. It has won awards, among them a Saltire Society Housing Design Award 2015 and the Royal Institute of British Architects (RIBA) House of the Year 2016.

Hidden not far away, down Dublin Street Lane North, is the village-like Dublin Street Lane Housing (Richard Murphy Architects 2000). The context is a historically significant site surrounded by New Town tenements. This was Broughton Village, in a rural landscape before the New Town was built. Murphy's village, oriented on the old hamlet's footprint, evokes the lost vernacular character.

94
Physicians' Hall
9 Queen Street
Thomas Hamilton 1846

The Royal College of Physicians was established in 1681 in the Old Town, where the physicians funded a free dispensary for the poor, the first such public service in Britain, subsidised by treating those who could pay. When those who could pay began to move to the New Town the physicians followed. They hired James Craig in 1775 to design a meeting place. Craig was well known as the architect of the New Town Plan, for which the Magistrates of Edinburgh in 1767 awarded him a gold medal with the Freedom of the City in a silver box, but he gained few commissions thereafter. His Physicians' Hall, a dignified classical building, was one of only a few designs to flow from his pen. Financial issues forced the physicians to sell it in 1843 (see 97).

The proceeds funded this Greco-Roman palazzo. Its statues (Alexander Handyside Ritchie sculptor) represent Hygeia goddess of health, Asclepius god of medicine and Hippocrates of the Hippocratic Oath. Opulent interior; also a courtyard garden recalling the Edinburgh Physic Garden, established at Holyrood in 1670 by Robert Sibbald and Andrew Balfour, who were among the founders of the college. Their garden was the genesis of Edinburgh's Royal Botanic Garden (see 144–149).

95
Standard Life Building
1 George Street
JM Dick Peddie & George Washington Browne
c. 1900
Standard Life was founded in Edinburgh in 1825 as The Life Insurance Company of Scotland. It grew to have offices and agents around the world. This Palladian headquarters represented that success. The pediment's figurative group symbolises financial planning, its theme appropriated from the parable 'The Wise and Foolish Virgins'. The foolish are in distress; the wise worry-free. The design reprised a tableau by sculptor John Steell on the previous façade (David Bryce 1839) which could not be salvaged. The symbolism surfaced again on the expressive bronze frieze (Gerald Laing artist) running along the top of the adjoining office building (Michael Laird & Partners 1978), also for Standard Life.

96
St Andrew's Church
13 George Street
Major Andrew Frazer 1784; steeple 1787
The first church built in the New Town, following a competition for it held by the town council. It would have faced St Andrew Square had the site there

not been pre-empted (see 89). The elliptical plan was architect and Royal Engineer Frazer's response to the unintended location. The galleried interior has an Adamesque plaster ceiling, stained glass by Ballantine, and two windows by 20th-century masters of the craft (Alfred Webster 1913; Douglas Strachan 1934). The entrance is a Roman Corinthian portico. The original bells (Whitechapel Bell Foundry, London 1788) are in the tower, which is decorated with garlands and a ghostly mask of Father Time above the clock.

In 1843, St Andrew's was where the Reverend Thomas Chalmers led the 'great schism' – the Disruption of the Church of Scotland – which resulted in 450 ministers across the country walking out. They were protesting that ministers be elected by the people, not appointed by landowners. Architects benefited when the rebels set up their own 'free kirks'. The dissidents from St Andrew's later worshipped at St George's Free Church (see 125). The congregations were subsequently reunited. St Andrew's is now called St Andrew's and St George's West Church.

97

The Dome

14 George Street

David Rhind 1847

The Commercial Bank of Scotland bought James Craig's Physicians' Hall and demolished it to make way for this Greco-Roman temple bank. Its majestic Corinthian portico is crowned with a pediment featuring Navigation, Agriculture, Justice, Caledonia (the central figure), Enterprise, Merchandise and Science (Alexander Handyside Ritchie sculptor). The building was later a branch of the Royal Bank of Scotland. A double-height foyer leads to the former banking hall. Its dome inspired the name of the bar and restaurant that opened here after RBS moved out in 1993.

The design was recreated contemporaneously as the head office of the Bank of Montreal, the 'Scots' bank in Canada, whose building committee had requested drawings of suitable 'banking houses' from contacts in Scotland.

98

Capital Building

12–13 St Andrew Square

Leslie Grahame Thomson & Frank James Connell

1939

A gust of Nordic air to refresh the Caledonian Insurance Company, previously at 19 George Street (now a hotel). Architect Connell visited Scandinavia in 1934 and the influence of that region's transition to modernism is evident in the building's traditional but austere form and granite-clad façades. The naked, bronze figures (Alexander Carrick sculptor) on columns flanking the entrance symbolise 'safety and domestic bliss'. They resemble the work of Norwegian sculptor Gustav Vigeland which Connell would have seen in Oslo.

99

Jenners Department Store Building

47–48 Princes Street

William Hamilton Beattie (George Beattie & Son) 1895

Jenners was named after co-founder Charles Jenner, a linen draper. The first store was established in 1837, in a row of converted Georgian houses. It was destroyed by fire in 1892. From the ashes rose this palazzo of Victorian consumerism, constructed to be 'fireproof' with cement and granite composite floor slabs, steel beams and iron columns. A corner dome was sketched but not fitted. The façades are a cornucopia of ornament and sculpture (William Birnie Rhind) including figures symbolising nature's four seasons and 12 caryatids in various national costumes. Jenner specified female forms to emphasise that women shoppers sustained his business.

The belle-époque extravaganza was promoted as 'The Most Fashionable Shopping Centre in Scotland', the 'Harrods of the North'. There were more than 60 departments, lit by electric lights and served by elevators. Wrought iron gates are decorated with thistles and Charles Jenner's monogram. The store was extended on South St David Street (Andrew Robb Scott 1903). Inside is the original timber- and glass-roofed, galleried atrium. A proposal to transform the interior as a hotel was revealed in 2019.

100
Scott Monument
East Princes Street Gardens
George Meikle Kemp 1840–6
No one did more to create the image of Scotland as a land of lochs, castles and tartan-clad chieftains than Walter Scott. His *Waverley* novels were bestsellers. His monument is the tallest in the world dedicated to a writer.

Scott's biographer and son-in-law, JG Lockhart, suggested it be 'a huge Homeric cairn' on top of Arthur's Seat. Princes Street Gardens prevailed. A competition was held. The winner was self-taught architect George Meikle Kemp. His flying-buttressed Gothic rocket – rising 61 metres with 287 steps to the top – was inspired by Gothic cathedrals in northern France which he had visited in 1824, and Melrose Abbey which he admired (as did Scott). Some of the competition entries were classical, appropriate for the 'Athens of the North' (William Playfair's drawing of 1835 shows a lofty obelisk), but Gothic is closer to the medieval spirit of Scott.

The monument is decorated with statues representing characters from his novels and Scottish history. The biggest is Scott himself, seated with a book and his deerhound, carved from a single block of Carrara marble (John Steell sculptor). The marble shines against a patchwork of old and new stones: the old blackened by soot from steam trains at Waverley Station; the new from conservation deliberately not disguised.

Kemp was not at the inauguration in 1846. He drowned in the Union Canal on a foggy night in 1844. His brother-in-law, William Bonnar, supervised the monument's completion. It has outlived all criticism (Charles

Dickens said it looked like 'the spire of a Gothic church taken off and stuck on the ground'). Many artists made sculptures for it, among them Amelia Hill, a woman in the Victorian art world that was dominated by men (her husband was David Octavius Hill; see 78). She designed the David Livingstone Monument (1875), which stands in the shadow of Scott's rocket. It shows the missionary and explorer standing above the head of the lion that once attacked him.

Edinburgh's other Scott monument is Corstorphine Hill Tower (1871), above Edinburgh Zoo. It was erected by enthusiast William Macfie of Clermiston to mark the centenary of the writer's birth. The world's first monument to Scott, a mighty classical column supporting a statue of him, was erected in Glasgow in 1837–8.

101
Playfair Steps
The Mound
William Playfair 1828

The Mound is a massive earthwork made with soil and rock removed to prepare the site of the New Town for development. It crosses what was the Nor Loch, a lake created in the 15th century for defence below Castle Rock. The loch, picturesque from afar, was polluted with rubbish and effluent from the Old Town. In 1759, Lord Provost George

Drummond ordered it drained. William Playfair fashioned the fill as a classical landscape on which he built the Royal Scottish Academy, the Scottish National Gallery and the Mound Steps, which carry his name.

At the top of the steps is his Gothic Free Church College of 1846 (the

theological college built for the Free Church of Scotland after the Disruption of 1843), now the University of Edinburgh's School of Divinity. To the east, is the baroque cliff face of the Bank of Scotland (see 62) and, on land donated by the bank, the Black Watch Memorial (William Birnie Rhind sculptor 1910).

In the college quadrangle is a statue of John Knox (John Hutchison sculptor 1896) preaching like a prophet, a bible in his left hand. In 1972, the steps were renamed 'John Knox Way' to mark 400 years since the death of the Protestant reformer. But there were

no steps in Knox's time. A campaign by the Cockburn Association led to them being renamed for their architect in 1978.

102
Goose Pie House (Ramsay Lodge)
Ramsay Garden

Former home of poet Allan Ramsay and his artist son, portrait painter Allan Ramsay. Ramsay *père*, a nationalist and Jacobite, ran a bookshop by St Giles' Kirk where, in 1725, he set up the city's first circulating library. Religious zealots denounced him for corrupting folk with 'villainous, profane and obscene books and plays lent out for an easy price.' His house, Ramsay Lodge (1734), was likened by contemporary wits to a goose pie because of its octagonal shape. It was later enclosed by Ramsay Garden (see 54). A statue of the poet is at the foot of The Mound (John Steell sculptor 1865).

103
Royal Scottish Academy
The Mound
> *William Playfair 1822–6;*
> *extended 1831–6*
> **103.1**
Scottish National Gallery
> *William Playfair 1850–55*

Two Greek Revival art galleries sited by Playfair for scenic effect on The Mound. Their style cemented the city's claim to be the 'Athens of the North', with culture at the core of civic life.

The Royal Scottish Academy (RSA), founded in 1826, evolved from the Royal Institution for the Encouragement of the Fine Arts in Scotland. Its building, with a huge Doric portico on Princes Street, was home to the Board of Manufactures & Fisheries (which commissioned it) and the Royal Society and the Society of Antiquaries. In 1850, construction started on a purpose built RSA building sited directly south. The academicians shared it with the newly formed National Gallery of Scotland, which took it over when the academicians returned to their original premises in 1911.

Playfair aligned the original RSA to command the view from Hanover Street, and later composed the two towers of Free Church College on the axis; the architects of Tolbooth St John's Church (see 56) followed suit (the National Gallery is also in step with the alignment). The RSA building is heavy with fluted Doric columns and Grecian ornament, sphinxes and a colossal statue of Queen Victoria (John Steell sculptor 1844). The National Gallery is

elegant with Ionic rather than Doric columns. Much of budget for it was spent on engineering, the site being above railway tunnels under The Mound.

When planning the National Gallery, Playfair drew it and the RSA rising from woodland in Princes Street

Gardens, not as now from a plaza. The open space was part of the 'Playfair Project' (John Miller & Partners 1999–2004), which added an underground link between the buildings, more display space, a lecture theatre, shop and restaurant. Subsequent work at the National Gallery, to better display the collection of Scottish art, started in 2018 (Hoskins Architects).

104
The New Club
86 Princes Street
In 1967, Scotland's oldest private members' club, founded in 1787, demolished its heritage build-ing on Princes Street for this reinforced concrete, granite-clad design (Alan Reiach, Eric Hall & Partners, Blyth and Blyth engineers 1969). The club's wood panelled dining room (Robert Lorimer c.1910) was salvaged and reinstated within the new building.

Above the shops on the ground floor is a cantilevered walkway that goes nowhere. The promenade evolved from the Abercrombie Plan, a post-war initiative to make Edinburgh a 'city for tomorrow'. A motorway would have been ploughed through the city centre and Princes Street rebuilt. In 1954, the 'Princes Street Panel' was set up to consider specific options. A continu-ous walkway to separate people from traffic was proposed. Every old build-ing would have been replaced with New Club lookalikes. Some were built and several Victorian buildings lost before the plan was abandoned in 1982. Ironically, the radical idea to reconstruct Princes Street was consistent with the uniformity of James Craig's New Town Plan of 1767.

The Abercrombie plan was not the first in Edinburgh to provoke outrage. Henry Cockburn, in his 1849 'Letter to The Lord Provost on the Best Ways of Spoiling The Beauty of Edinburgh', recalled as 'absolutely insane' a proposal to build houses along the south side of Princes Street, 'utterly and forever cutting off the view of the Old Town.' The town council had already allowed the site of what is now the Balmoral Hotel to be developed. An Act of Parlia-ment (1816) was required to prevent more construction and to protect the view across Princes Street Gardens. The open space was part of the New Town Plan and is its genius and glory.

105
The Merchants' Hall
22 Hanover Street
David Bryce junior 1866;
MacGibbon & Ross 1879

Opened as the Edinburgh branch of the City of Glasgow Bank. The north half was built first and features a Renaissance-style banking hall and skylit dome. The bank crashed catastrophically in 1878. Its directors were tried at Edinburgh's High Court and found guilty of fraud.

The unfinished palazzo was bought in 1879 by and adapted for the Company of Merchants of the City of Edinburgh (decorative symbols of its activities were added to the banking hall). The south wing planned in 1866 was completed in 1901 (Thomas P Marwick). In the Secretary and Chamberlain's room is an oil painting showing receipt of the company's Charter of Incorporation from Charles II in 1681. On the front porch is the merchants' heraldry and motto: *Terraque Marique*, meaning 'by land and sea'.

106
The Royal Society of Edinburgh
22–26 George Street

The society was founded in 1783 to promote 'the advancement of learning and useful knowledge'. It occupies the former Edinburgh Life Assurance Company premises (David Bryce 1843) and the company's subsequent Edwardian baroque headquarters (JM Dick Peddie 1909), where the figure of Prudence still stands on the dome.

Period interiors remain in the Victorian building, where portraits of past Presidents of the Society, among them Walter Scott, are displayed. It was here, after the novelist's death in 1832, that the idea of a monument to him was first discussed, and a public meeting to promote it arranged at the Assembly Rooms. Outside the Royal Society is the Monument to George IV (Francis Chantrey sculptor 1831), erected to commemorate the monarch's visit to Edinburgh in 1822 (see 113).

107
Assembly Rooms
54 George Street
John Henderson 1784–7; William
Burn (portico) 1818; internal
additions by Burn and David Bryce

The most important surviving 18th-century building of its type in Scotland, of special significance to the New Town. The name comes from Assembly Close, where the Old Town's wealthy residents gathered at 'assemblies' to dance and party. When they flitted to the New Town, a new building was required. The city donated the land; public subscription paid for the venue which opened with high society attending the Caledonian Hunt Ball.

For two centuries, social and cultural gatherings have been held under the crystal galaxy of chandeliers in the ballroom. George IV's attendance in 1822 caused a traffic jam of horse-drawn carriages on George Street. Edinburgh Festival events have been held here since the festival started in 1947. The opulent interiors were recently upgraded and heritage features restored (LDN Architects 2015).

108
St Stephen's Stockbridge
105 St Stephen Street
William Playfair 1828

Gigantic classical church with an octagonal 'great hall' and 50-metre high clock tower designed to command the view down Howe Street – an example of Playfair's urban design, with a twist.

The town council had considered the site for a public school to serve the second (northern) New Town, but decided instead to relocate the Royal High School (see 74) from the Old Town to Calton Hill, where the eastern New Town (planned by Playfair in 1819) was being built. However, a rival to the Royal High appeared – The Edinburgh Academy (William Burn 1824), a private school which still stands on Henderson Row. The city's revenge, so the story goes, was to allow St Stephen's Church to block the academy's Greek Revival-style façade from view.

109
Robert Louis Stevenson House
17 Heriot Row
Robert Reid & William Sibbald c. 1808

The New Town was planned as a residential suburb for the well-to-do and built, initially, to stringent design controls. It has since been defiled by piecemeal commercial development. The second New Town, north of Queen Street, is largely unspoiled. Heriot Row is characteristic: a wide street of well-proportioned townhouses, aristocratic but not pompous. It was named for George Heriot's Trust whose governors invested in land here.

On the wall of Number 17 is a stone engraved with the words 'The Home of Robert Louis Stevenson 1857–80'. The last verse of his poem 'The Lamplighter' is inscribed on a brass plate by the street light where, in the gloaming, the young Stevenson, looking out, saw the gas lamp being lit. Across the street is Queen Street Gardens where he played. There is a pond with an island, an inspiration, it is speculated, for his novel *Treasure Island*.

110
Northern Lighthouse Board
84 George Street

The façade (1788) looks as it was in 1832 when the Northern Lighthouse Board, founded in 1786, opened its headquarters here. Among the NLB's employees were Robert Louis Stevenson's grandfather, Robert Stevenson, and father, Thomas Stevenson, both lighthouse engineers.

Robert Stevenson was the engineer of the Melville Monument (see 88). He is best known as the designer of the legendary Bell Rock lighthouse (1811) which warns mariners of a treacherous reef in the North Sea. The model lighthouse above the fanlight at the entrance symbolises the NLB's founding purpose: to protect mariners from shipwreck. The model was made in the workshop once here and installed in 1950.

111

78-80 George Street

John James Burnet 1903–7

Edwardian exuberance in Burnet's commercial style, with twin domes, Italianate eaves gallery and baroque details. The caryatid-style figures (attributed to sculptor William Birnie Rhind) represent the four seasons. Ionic columns rise through two floors. The façade completely disrupts the Georgian streetscape, but what a way to do it.

The client was the Professional & Civil Service Supply Association, a co-op for white-collar workers. This was its department store. The Scottish Co-operative Wholesale Society took it over in 1936. The interior was gutted for offices in 1972. The original marble and bronze storefront and the twin columns at the entrance, removed by the SCWS, were replicated in fibreglass.

The rear elevation in Rose Street North Lane is remarkable – a proto-modernist vertical grid of glazed white brick and glass to maximise daylight inside.

112

Royal Scots Greys Memorial

West Princes Street Gardens

William Birnie Rhind 1906

On a rocky pedestal, a bronze statue of a Scots Greys trooper with carbine and wearing the regimental bearskin cap. It is the most striking of three military memorials in the city by Birnie Rhind: the others honour the King's Own Scottish Borderers (1906, on North Bridge) and the Black Watch (1910, on The Mound). The primary plaque shows the Scots Grey's eagle insignia (see 57).

There are other army monuments in the gardens. The most unexpected is Wojtek the Bear (Alan Herriot sculptor 2015), on the path west of the Scots Grey's Memorial. The bear was adopted by soldiers of a Polish unit in the Second World War and was their mascot during the Italian Campaign. After the war, the Poles were demobbed in Scotland, along with the bear which became an attraction at Edinburgh Zoo.

113
Walter Scott's Townhouse
39 North Castle Street

Palatial façade originally fronting three townhouses (39–43 North Castle Street), now offices. The homes, built in 1793, were among the earliest in the New Town and, externally, show the architectural quality aspired to at the time. From 1802 until 1826, Walter Scott lived at number 39. It was here that he choreographed the visit to Edinburgh in 1822 of George IV (the first by a reigning monarch to Scotland since Charles II).

King George took in what tourists see today, but with pageantry. The visit was significant for its royal rehabilitation of tartan. Wearing it had been banned by the Act of Proscription after the Jacobite rising of 1745 (the military allowed tartan, to encourage recruitment to Highland regiments). The act was repealed in 1782. By then, the Jacobite threat to the Hanoverian crown had been eliminated. Highlanders, previously feared, found themselves romanticised, thanks to Scott.

He defended Scotland's distinct society and spent a lifetime promoting his version of it. He sent invitations to clan chieftains to attend the 1822 ceremonies in full Highland dress. George IV, convinced by Scott that he was the heir to a noble tradition, wore the Royal Stuart tartan. The 'King's Jaunt', as writer John Prebble called it, had a lasting effect – every trader selling tartan souvenirs on the Royal Mile today can be grateful for it.

Scott's stature and that of other writers associated with Edinburgh led to the city being declared in 2004 the world's first UNESCO City of Literature.

114
Church of Scotland Offices
121 George Street
Sydney Mitchell & Wilson 1911

'Florentine in feeling' said *The Scotsman*, referring to the building's eaves gallery and arcade; also Scandinavian in the austere reworking of these Renaissance features. The asymmetrical façade is due to a 1933 addition required after the union in 1929 of the United Free Church and the Church of Scotland (an extension to balance the elevation was not built). Above the entrance is a vigorous rendering in bronze of the Kirk's coat of arms: the Burning Bush flanked by angels, the Dove of Peace and Noah's Ark. Also bronze is the elaborate escutcheon for flagpoles.

Nearby, at the intersection of George Street and Castle Street, is a statue of the founding Moderator of the General Assembly of the Free Church of Scotland, Thomas Chalmers (John Steell sculptor 1878).

115
The Oxford Bar
8 Young Street
John Young c. 1780

No frills back-alley bar thought to have been a public house since 1811, originally residential. Its builder, John Young, was the first property developer in the New Town. He built 1–2 Thistle Court, semi-detached dwellings on Thistle Street, three blocks east of here. It was the first house built in the New Town. James Craig laid the foundation stone for it in 1767, but there is no record that he designed it.

The Oxford Bar is famous for its association with Detective John Rebus and his creator, writer Ian Rankin. Where did it get its name? Nobody, not even Rebus, knows for sure. Purpose? Stand-up drinking, seating limited.

116

1–11 Charlotte Square

Robert Adam 1791; completed 1805

Robert Adam, the go-to architect for sophisticated splendour, was hired by the town council to raise the profile of Charlotte Square. He drew a neoclassical 'palace front', one of the last designs in his portfolio. After he died in 1792, the council ensured, on the north side at least, that those who completed the work respected the master's plan.

The façade is an illusion intended to look like a monumental mansion. It conceals 11 townhouses (nine in front, one on each side), each with its own entrance. The raised stones by the roadside outside the houses allowed residents and visitors to board or descend with ease from horse-drawn carriages. The apartments attracted a who's who of aristocratic buyers. Number 5 and, subsequently, number 6 were the city homes of the 4th Marquess of Bute who restored the properties (and number 7) between 1903 and 1927. Number 7, the Georgian House, was restored (c. 1975) by the National Trust for Scotland and furnished in period style to show how the first owner, a Highland clan chieftain, John Lamont and his family, lived in luxury upstairs; downstairs were the kitchen and servants' areas, also restored.

Six Charlotte Square, known as Bute House, is the official residence of the First Minister of the Scottish Government. Like many properties in the New Town, it is inhabited by ghosts of slavery. The Legacies of British Slave-ownership database cites this address being associated with claimants of compensation after legislation in 1833 outlawed slave-ownership in British colonies.

117
Prince Albert Memorial
Charlotte Square

John Steell sculptor 1876

In the middle of Charlotte Square gardens, an elegiac, bronze equestrian statue in memory of Prince Albert. Planning to completion took more than a decade – every detail of the design had to be approved by the widowed Queen Victoria. Several sites were proposed by the executive committee, which favoured a ridge above St Margaret's Loch (appropriate because the loch was Prince Albert's idea, to beautify Holyrood Park). *The Scotsman* published letters from readers who doubted the prince would have approved of any man-made object in that landscape. Eventually, Charlotte Square was chosen.

The prince is dressed as an honorary field marshal. Narrative panels – notably the royal couple opening the Great Exhibition of 1851, of which the prince was patron – are on the granite pedestal (David Bryce architect). Around it are figurative groups (by several sculptors) of society in mourning. The monument was unveiled by the queen. Sculptor John Steell was knighted at Holyroodhouse.

On the west side of the square is the former St George's Church (1811–14) terminating the view from George Street (a church on this site was part of James Craig's New Town Plan). The original design was sketched in 1791 by Robert Adam. Four neoclassical cupolas were to have risen at each corner of the structure, to frame the dome. The elaborate composition was diluted by Adam's successor, Robert Reid. St George's closed in 1961 due to prohibitive costs of repair. The congregation merged with St Andrew's Church (see 96). The building was converted (1968–70) as West Register House, to augment General Register House (see 81). The interior was gutted and replaced by five floors for offices and storage of public archives.

Charlotte Square was marked 'St George's Square' on Craig's New Town Plan. The name was changed in 1785, either because there already was a George Square (see 207) or because Charlotte was the name of George III's queen and first daughter. The gardens traditionally host the annual Edinburgh International Book Festival (the event went online in 2020 due to the Covid-19 pandemic).

118

Moray Place

James Gillespie Graham
1822–36

The Earl of Moray imposed strict rules on buyers of his feued lots, to conform to architect Gillespie Graham's grand plan for the Moray estate. Its architec-

tural apotheosis is this neoclassical circus in the style of Robert Adam. All the features for which Georgian architecture and urbanism in the New Town are admired are here: finely cut stonework on façades punctuated with columns and pediments in Greek Revival style; cast iron lamp posts, railings and anthemion-patterned balconies; sash windows, and main doors with elegant fanlights; cupola-lit stairwells and spacious apartments decorated originally in Adamesque style.

The circus which the townhouses overlook remains paved with granite setts. The façades are saved from monotony by rhythmic articulation of the pediments and columns, and the fortuitous lie of the land which slopes gently. There is a private garden for residents, an enviable and characteristic feature of Craig's New Town Plan.

The Royal Botanic Garden Edinburgh

The Botanics can be traced back to a 17th century physic garden near Holyrood Abbey where medicinal herbs and plants were grown. Since the 1820s, the RBGE has been based at Inverleith, a former country estate. Its picturesque 70-acre landscape has evolved with a diverse range of trees and plants from around the world. No botanical or, indeed, architectural enthusiast visiting the city should miss it.

The diversity extends to buildings and structures. These range from a Georgian mansion (Inverleith House) and an eco-friendly 21st-century visitor centre (John Hope Gateway) to the garden's outstanding array of glasshouses, among them the Modern Alpine House and the Temperate Palm House (above), a classic of the Victorian era.

3

The West End & Inverleith

The Ross Fountain—St John's Church—Caledonian Railway Hotel—
Edinburgh International Conference Centre—Usher Hall—St Mary's
Episcopal Cathedral—Donaldson's School—Scottish National Gallery
of Modern Art—Stewart's Melville College—Dean Cemetery—Dean
Village—St Bernard's Well—Stockbridge Colonies—Royal Botanic
Garden—Fettes College—Maggie's Centre . . .

119

The Ross Fountain

West Princes Street Gardens

Antoine Durenne Foundry c. 1869

Beaux-Arts cast iron fountain similar to one erected at the 1862 International Exhibition in London, which Edinburgh gunsmith Daniel Ross saw. He proposed to the city a copy to beautify Princes Street Gardens.

It was cast in France and its 122 pieces shipped to Leith. What Leith's dock workers thought of the fountain's mermaids, female figures symbolising arts and sciences, lion masks, dolphins and naked water nymph is not recorded. The Reverend Ramsay, minister at St John's Church near where the fountain appeared in 1872, declared the nymph on top of the fountain 'grossly indecent; offensive to the moral feelings of the community.' But he was soon dead and the fountain stayed. Ross died before seeing water flow from it. It is his memorial. Ramsay was honoured with a Celtic cross (Robert Rowand Anderson 1879) facing Princes Street outside his church.

In 2017, the fountain was removed for a piece-by-piece repair (Industrial Heritage Consulting; Lost Art restoration) commissioned by the Ross Development Trust, the city and Edinburgh World Heritage. It was reassembled in 2018, repainted with a 19th-century French colour scheme.

120
St John's Church
Princes Street at Lothian Road
William Burn 1818

Perpendicular Gothic with pinnacles, buttresses, and a tower which would have been taller had its lantern not collapsed in a gale before the church was completed. The nave is lined with pillars which bloom, like daffodils, with glorious fan-vaulting. The altar has a mosaic triptych (1889) in Pre-Raphaelite style. Stained glass windows are mostly by the Ballantine studio (c. 1860). The nave and chancel were redecorated and brightly lit (Benjamin Tindall Architects 2001); the chandeliers were based on those at The Hub (see 56). Also of note is the congenial Cornerstone community centre (LDN Architects 2018).

Nearby is St Cuthbert's Church, on Edinburgh's oldest ecclesiastical site where Celtic missionary St Cuthbert founded a chapel in the 7th century. In 1130, David I assigned it to Holyrood Abbey. The present building (Hippolyte Blanc 1894), with a baroque elevation facing Princes Street Gardens, incorporates the Georgian tower and spire of its predecessor.

Both churches have atmospheric graveyards. There is a walled enclosure at St John's built to deter grave robbers; at St Cuthbert's there is a watch-tower (1827) for the same purpose. The robbers, called 'Resurrectionists', sold bodies for anatomy lessons at the University of Edinburgh. The Anatomy Act of 1832 put the body-snatchers out of business, by legalising the sale of corpses to medical schools. Among the burials at St Cuthbert's is George Meikle Kemp, architect of the Scott Monument.

121

Caledonian Railway Hotel

Lothian Road at Princes Street

Kinnear & Peddie 1890–3;
JM Dick Peddie & George
Washington Browne 1899–1903

Princes Street station opened in 1848 in a simple timber structure, later a single-storey Beaux-Arts building by Kinnear & Peddie to which was added, around 1900, several floors and a mansard roof in French Renaissance style. This was the Caledonian Railway Hotel, built to compete with the North British Hotel (see 80).

The Caley's *fin de siècle* château arrived with the architectural panache of Victorian Glasgow. Its Dumfriesshire red sandstone was commonly used in the city of the west where the company was based. Allegorical figures of Engineering, Agriculture, Commerce and the Arts are enthroned above the entrance; the pediment displays the Caley's coat of arms flanked by figures representing the railway as a force of speed and progress (John Hutchison sculptor 1894). The station closed in 1965. The concourse survives, re-roofed to create an atrium for the hotel, now the Waldorf Astoria. The iron and glass train shed was demolished. The station's cast iron and timber gateway on Rutland Street was restored to its original colours in 2018. The railway right-of-way into the West End is easily traced: it is now the West Approach Road.

122

Edinburgh International Conference Centre

150 Morrison Street

Terry Farrell & Partners 1995

Animated with sail-like canopies, a glass curtain wall revealing the foyer, and a steel cornice illuminated like a halo at night, this by far the most likable of the Exchange Financial District's postmodern buildings. The district, master-planned by Terry Farrell & Partners, occupies the former Caledonian Railway yards. The Conference Centre would have been better placed on Festival Square across from the Usher Hall, but the Sheraton Hotel was already there.

The square is an arid public space. Proposed for the site is a new venue for Edinburgh Filmhouse and the Film Festival (Richard Murphy Architects), endorsed by and named for movie star and local hero Sean Connery.

123
Usher Hall
Lothian Road
> *Stockdale Harrison & Sons*
> *and Howard Henry Thomson*
> *architects, Redpath, Brown*
> *& Co. engineers 1910–14*

Prestigious city-owned concert hall funded by brewer and whisky distilling magnate Andrew Usher. George V and Queen Mary laid the foundation stone. Sculptures of female figures on the façade symbolise the joy of music (one holds a model of the building). The Beaux-Arts composition conceals a reinforced concrete and steel structure. The dome is a stylistic conceit: the auditorium below it is not circular but horseshoe-shaped. A three-level extension to the foyer, in harmony with the radius of the dome, is defined externally not with fake stone but with a glazed curtain wall – a clear distinction between the old and the new (LDN Architects, Will Rudd Davidson engineers, Speirs + Major lighting design 2009).

Adjacent are the Royal Lyceum Theatre, (Charles J Phipps 1883), a Victorian classic, and the Traverse Theatre (Groves-Raines Architects 1992) with an entrance rotunda echoing the curve of the Usher Hall.

124
Rutland Square
Archibald Elliot 1830s
At the end of Rutland Street is one of the city's most intimate and best preserved squares. Its architecture and urban design follow precedents in the New Town. Here can be found the Scottish Arts Club, established in 1873 in the West End (at 24 Rutland Square since 1894) and The Royal Incorporation of Architects in Scotland (number 15). The RIAS, founded in 1916, was gifted its property by founder and first president Robert Rowand Anderson, whose townhouse it was.

125

Charlotte Chapel

58 Shandwick Place

David Bryce 1869

Former St George's West, originally St George's Free Church. Muscular Roman baroque, to which was added a clock and bell tower (Robert Rowand Anderson 1881), inspired by the *campanile* at San Giorgio Maggiore, Venice (essentially, this is Anderson's unbuilt tower for the University of Edinburgh's Medical School; see 158). Baroque interior refurbished (Lee Boyd Architects 2016) for a Baptist congregation; 'Charlotte' refers to its previous chapel (1816) on Rose Street, near Charlotte Square.

126

Gladstone Monument

Coates Crescent

James Pittendrigh Macgillivray 1910; unveiled 1917 on St Andrew Square

Baroque glorification of Liberal Member of Parliament for Midlothian and four-time Prime Minister William Ewart Gladstone. Around him are allegorical figures representing Faith (with Bible), Measure (with yard stick), Fortitude (Crown of Thorns) and Vitality (Lamp of Life); seated figures represent History (hooded) and Eloquence. Two boys hold a laurel wreath; banners quote Homer's *The Iliad*. Three birds of prey recall the family name 'Gledstane' (not thought related to the same at Gladstone's Land; see 59).

The monument, declared a hazard to traffic on St Andrew Square, was moved here in 1955, the site for which it was designed but not installed when Tory property owners nearby objected to having it in their park. What should have caused outrage – and would now – is Gladstone's link to slavery. His father, Leith-born John Gladstone, owned plantations worked by African slaves in the West Indies. The Gladstones gained a fortune in government compensation after the abolition of slave ownership in 1833.

127

Edinburgh Trades House, 'Ashfield'

61 Melville Street

Robert Brown 1861

Melville Street is the principal axis of the
western New Town, developed (1825–70) by
Patrick Walker whose estate it was. This end-of-terrace address has, since
1971, been the headquarters of Edinburgh Trades House. The organisation
evolved from the Incorporated Trades of Edinburgh in the Old Town, the
governance and development of which the trades influenced. There is a museum, accessible by appointment. It is one of the city's hidden treasures.

128

West End Medical Practice

36 Manor Place

Page\Park Architects 2014

The practice moved from a gloomy
ground floor and basement in a nearby
19th-century terrace to this stylish
contemporary addition to the West End townscape. The low-rise building is
bright, eco-friendly and a good neighbour to St Mary's Cathedral, in whose
grounds it was built. It is transparent and welcoming on a freshly landscaped
site, and there is a green roof. The front curves to avoid mature trees; new
plantings compensate for those that had to be felled.

129

Arthur Conan Doyle Centre

25 Palmerston Place

John Lessels 1881

Arthur Conan Doyle, the creator of Sherlock
Holmes, never lived here but he was born in
Edinburgh. His interest in spiritualism inspired the name of centre, home of
The Edinburgh Association of Spiritualists since 2011. The original owner was
brewery baron William McEwan, for whom the French roof was added and
the interior remodelled in 1886. The adjoining terrace on Palmerston Place
has Glasgow-style bay windows, common in late Victorian Edinburgh.

130

St Mary's Episcopal Cathedral

Palmerston Place

George Gilbert Scott, John Oldrid Scott 1874–91; Charles Oldrid Scott (west spires) 1913–17

Funded by a bequest from sisters Barbara and Mary Walker who inherited the land and stipulated a cathedral be built. George Gilbert Scott was awarded the commission after a competition in 1872. Entries, three from Scottish, three from English architects, were anonymous. Scott was English. His submission came with a cheeky nom de plume – 'Auld Lang Syne'.

After Scott died in 1878, the work devolved to his son, John Oldrid Scott, who faithfully followed his father's plans. The medieval-style interior has outstanding decorative features: reredos (J Oldrid Scott) with an image of the Cross at Calvary flanked by Saint Columba and Saint (Queen) Margaret; a suspended Rood Cross (Robert Lorimer 1922) with Christ shown crucified on a background of Flanders poppies made for but not installed at the National War Memorial (see 52); and the radiant Millennium Window (Eduardo Paolozzi 2002) composed of three lancets and a rose which bathe the Resurrection Chapel (south transept) with coloured light.

The central tower with a spire is 90 metres high, which makes St Mary's the tallest building in Edinburgh. The weight of the tower was distributed to pillars, arches and buttresses to create column-free space directly below. The two towers and spires on the west front were an afterthought by the client,

lifted either from Scott's 'plan B', which he withdrew, or from the competition's second-placed entry (Alexander Ross), which lost by one vote. They were completed by Scott's grandson, Charles Oldrid Scott.

On the north side of the cathedral are Old Coates House (17th-century), Walpole Hall (Robert Lorimer 1933) and St Mary's Song School (J Oldrid Scott 1885). The interior of the Song School is decorated with glittering murals (1888–92) by Phoebe Traquair (see 92).

131
Heart of Midlothian Memorial Clock
Haymarket

Henry Snell Gamley 1922

Obelisk inscribed 'Erected by the Heart of Midlothian Football Club to the Memory of their Players and Members who fell in the Great War 1914–1919.' The Hearts team joined the 16th Royal Scots, known as McCrae's Battalion, in 1914. Its battle honours are inscribed here. A crowd of 35,000 attended the unveiling.

Nearby is the redesigned Haymarket Station (IDP Architects 2012–14). Its Victorian building (1842) was the booking hall and head office of the Edinburgh & Glasgow Railway. The station was the end of the line until 1846, when Haymarket Tunnel to Waverley Station was completed.

132
Donaldson's School
West Coates

William Playfair 1842–51

One of Edinburgh's 'pauper palaces', this one funded by the bequest of printer and publisher James Donaldson. It was called Donaldson's Hospital; like George Heriot's (see 43), 'hospital' meant a charitable institution, usually a school, this one for orphans and the 'deaf and disadvantaged'. The trustees said they liked Elizabethan architecture. Playfair was appointed, having submitted a design (in plan similar to Heriot's) that looked like 'somewhere Henry VIII might have met Anne Boleyn'.

In 2008, the school relocated. The site is now residential with a crescent of contemporary townhouses (Richard Murphy Architects 2019). These are set back behind the old school which was rehabilitated as flats. Murphy's interventions treated Playfair's architecture and its landscape setting with the respect they deserve.

133

Murrayfield Stadium

Roseburn Street

Home of the Scottish Rugby Union since 1925, originally with a stand on the west side and terraces where spectators stood whatever the weather. The cantilevered web of steel (Thorburn engineers 1992–4) provides wraparound cover in the now all-seat venue, capacity 67,500 fans. The maximum attendance, when Scotland beat Wales in 1975, was 104,000, a world record at the time. Outside is the War Memorial Arch (Rowand Anderson & Paul 1921), moved to Murrayfield from Inverleith where the previous ground was.

The world's first international rugby match (Scotland beat England) was played in 1871 on The Edinburgh Academy's ground, Raeburn Place, Stockbridge. The historic site has been transformed by a new stand (Michael Laird Architects 2020), designed to incorporate commercial space, recreational facilities and a Museum of International Rugby.

134

Pape's Cottages

1–3 Roseburn Cliff

A plaque on the south gable records the philanthropy of George Pape of Coltbridge House who funded the cottages (1894) 'for the use of three poor widows in all time coming' (the property is now a single family home). On the east gable is a plaque (1676) with the coat of arms of the Forresters of Corstorphine. The 17th-century-style gate pillars on Roseburn Terrace and the terrace of houses uphill were to have been part of Roseburn Cliff Garden Village (McArthy & Watson c.1902), promoted by Patrick Geddes but not completed.

Spanning the Water of Leith is Old Colt Bridge (1766), near where Hanoverian cavalry fled when Bonnie Prince Charlie's Jacobites approached Edinburgh in 1745, as a plaque on the parapet explains. The Water of Leith Walkway (access from Roseburn Cliff) leads to the galleries of modern art.

135
Scottish National Gallery of Modern Art, Modern One; 135.1 Modern Two
75 Belford Road

Two former charitable schools: Modern One, a Greek Revival design, was John Watson's Institution (William Burn 1825–8); Modern Two, in Italianate style, was Dean Orphanage (Thomas Hamilton 1831–3). Both are set in landscaped grounds, the experience of which is intensified by contemporary artworks.

The lawn at Modern One was transformed by *Landform*, a dreamy landscape inspired by natural forms and geological strata (Charles Jencks,

Terry Farrell & Partners, Ian White Associates 2001). The bronze figure surfacing from the pavement at the Belford Road is the first of six enigmatic humanoid sculptures sited between here and the sea, four of them in the Water of Leith (Antony Gormley 2010). A neon artwork, *Everything is going to be alright* (Martin Creed 2008), glows on Modern One's portico. On the lawn in

front of Modern Two is an illuminated text on scaffolding six metres high: *There Will Be No Miracles Here* (Nathan Coley 2009). The tension between the heritage buildings and the modern art in and around them is exhilarating.

There are no artworks on the portico at Modern Two, but above it is the clock salvaged from Netherbow Port (see 17). The interior was intelligently repurposed (Terry Farrell & Partners 1999), but the biggest personality here is not an architect but an artist – Leith-born Eduardo Paolozzi who gifted many works to the National Galleries. His studio has been reassembled and there is *Vulcan* (1999), a nine-metre tall, welded steel, pop art sculpture of the Roman god. The site-specific work dominates the double-height space where the café is located. Other major works by Paolozzi are at Edinburgh Park (see 282) and Picardy Place (top of Leith Walk).

136
St Andrew's Catholic Church
77 Belford Road
Timber-built church in the garden of Edge Hill House, a Victorian villa bought by the diocese as a clergy house. The Arts and Crafts-style church was built in 1902 for a growing suburban population. It was to have been temporary until a stone structure could be afforded. That proved unnecessary, it was so well-made, possibly from a kit of parts. Exterior with gabled porches, buttresses and board siding; half-timbering and bellcote on the west elevation. Atmospheric interior with wrought iron pendant lights with Saltire motif, and a timber trussed roof.

137
Stewart's Melville College
Queensferry Road
David Rhind 1849–55

Daniel Stewart endowed for orphaned and destitute boys a school to be managed by the Merchant Company (see 105). Architect Rhind submitted to the trustees three designs: one Italianate, one Gothic and this elaborate pageant of Elizabethan and Jacobean styles which was chosen. Inside is a modern performing arts centre designed to fit a former courtyard (Simpson & Brown Architects, David Narro Associates engineers 2007).

On Queensferry Road is Dean Park House, a lavish, French Second Empire-style mansion (Frederick Thomas Pilkington 1874) with bow windows for views to the north and a palatial porte cochère. It was built on land feued from the school, which acquired it in the 1960s. It is now the most ornate boarding house for schoolboys in Edinburgh.

138
Dean Cemetery
Dean Path

A who's who of 19th-century Scots in stone – academics, advocates, architects, artists, explorers and imperial army officers, inventors, physicians and philosophers. The memorials are a gazetteer of architectural styles, their decoration of exceptional artistic quality. The most ostentatious is the James Buchanan Monument (William Brodie sculptor), a *tempietto* like William Playfair's to Dugald Stewart on Calton Hill (page 58). Playfair himself is here, on 'Lords' Row' by the cemetery's west wall. His self-designed neoclassical tomb (1857) is next to the pyramid-shaped Rutherfurd Memorial, also his work (1852).

The cemetery was laid out in 1846 by architect David Cousin, on the site of the 16th-century Dean estate. He also designed the burial grounds at Warriston (1843), the first of Edinburgh's Victorian 'garden cemeteries', and Newington (1846). Like them, Dean Cemetery is open to the public (check times). The main gate is on Dean Path; another gate is in the car park at the National Galleries Modern Two.

139

Dean Village

Sydney Mitchell 1885

Grain milling was recorded in the 12th century in this steep-sided valley of the Water of Leith. By 1585, the town council was operating ten or so mills here. The village was further industrialised in the 19th century, with a whisky distillery, tannery and a chemical works; also slum housing.

John Ritchie Findlay, publisher of *The Scotsman*, could see the village from his townhouse at 3 Rothesay Terrace above the glen. He decided something should be done and hired architect Sydney Mitchell to improve the lives of the workers and their families. The model village designed for them is an architectural idyll, a blend of Arts and Crafts and 17th-century Scottish Renaissance styles.

140

Drumsheugh Baths

5 Belford Road

John James Burnet 1900

Moorish-style baths rebuilt by Burnet after his 1880s original burned down in 1892. The cast iron screens by the door spell out 'Drumsheugh Swimming and Turkish Baths Company', the oldest private baths in Edinburgh. Stairs lead down to the skylit pool which has a timber-framed roof supported by brick arches on cast iron columns. Restored and upgraded structurally (Lorn Macneal Architects, David Narro Associates engineers 2005). The baths are across the Water of Leith from Dean Village. The iron footbridge (1889) spans an old ford.

141

West Mill

24 Dean Path, Dean Village

The Incorporation of Baxters (bakers), one of the city's trades guilds, once operated several mills here, along the Water of Leith. This is the only one

left. The wheat sheaf on the gable is their symbol, applied when the mill was reconstructed (c. 1805). The mills declined in the late 19th century when steam power replaced water wheels and new mills were built at Leith.

On Bell's Brae, across the 18th-century bridge over the river, is the former Baxters' Granary. Above the blocked-up door is an eroded panel decorated with bakers' peels, scales, a sheaf of corn and cherub heads; also an inscription, 'God bless the Baxters of Edinburgh who built this House 1675.' The rubble-stone building, now harled, was converted as flats in the 1970s, as was West Mill. The bridge (which replaced a 16th-century, or earlier one) served the old road from Edinburgh to Queensferry. Downstream is Dean Bridge (1829–31), by the eminent engineer Thomas Telford, constructed for a new road and to open up land to the north for development.

Opposite West Mill is Dean School (Robert Wilson 1875), also now flats. On its façade is the Edinburgh School Board symbol: a roundel with the figure of Queen Margaret (personifying education), a pupil, globe and books.

142
St Bernard's Well
Water of Leith, Stockbridge
Alexander Nasmyth 1789

Mineral well discovered in 1760, reputedly by three schoolboys fishing. Advocate Lord Gardenstone adorned it with this picturesque Roman-style rotunda designed by Nasmyth (better known as a landscape painter) who had seen a similar structure at Tivoli. The Pump Room in the podium was decorated with mosaics in 1887 for publisher William Nelson who had bought the site, which he donated to the city. The statue on the podium is Hygeia, goddess of health (David Watson Stevenson sculptor 1887). A hopeful symbol, but the well was later closed, the water declared by the city's public health officer unsafe to drink.

143
Stockbridge Colonies
Glenogle Road

A self-help scheme begun in 1861 by seven stonemasons who formed the Edinburgh Co-operative Building Company, to build affordable housing and avoid exploitation by landlords. Stockbridge Colonies, originally called Glenogle Park, was the first of several similar ECBC projects, all of which survive. The co-op's members were artisan workers (panels on gable ends at Stockbridge illustrate their tools of trade). Investors received dividends; profits were reinvested to build more units for sale.

The typology – parallel rows of stone-built, slate-roofed terraces with ground floor flats accessed from one side and upper units reached by external stairs on the other – is unique to Edinburgh and Leith. The arrangement, unlike tenement living, gave each family a garden. The term 'colonies' came from the ECBC's policy of buying and 'colonising' marginal land.

144
Royal Botanic Garden Edinburgh (RBGE)
John Hope Gateway
Arboretum Road

Cullinan Studio, Buro Happold engineers, Gross. Max. landscape design 2009

Award-winning visitor centre named in honour of the 18th-century King's Botanist for Scotland and Regius Keeper of the Botanics, John Hope. It is a showcase of sustainable design. A wind turbine sprouts from the a green roof. Energy is generated from a biomass boiler and solar panels. Rainwater is harvested. Natural light and ventilation flow through the structure. Local materials were sourced where possible.

Wood is the big theme, visible throughout. The cross-laminated timber and glulam-beamed roof floats on slender steel columns; there is a helical timber staircase set in a skylit atrium; table tops in the restaurant are recycled timber from the garden; the building's rainscreen on Arboretum Road is larch. The garden side is a curved wall of glass, where exhibition space and the restaurant overlook a reflecting pool and biodiversity garden. A slate wall runs along the axis to Inverleith House, visually connecting the new building to its historic environment.

145

Inverleith House
Royal Botanic Garden
David Henderson 1774

Georgian mansion, originally the 'big house' of Inverleith estate. Part of the land was bought by the city in 1820 for the Botanics, at the time based at an increasingly urbanised Leith Walk. Inverleith offered clean air and open space. The Keeper of the garden lived in the house. The setting, with a view across the city to the Old Town, is unchanged. The Gallery of Modern Art occupied the house (1960–84). Public art in the Botanics includes a monument (1779) designed by Robert Adam, originally in the Leith Walk garden, commissioned by John Hope as homage to his friend and correspondent, Swedish botanist Carl Linnaeus. Inverleith Park (1889) was also part of Inverleith estate.

146

The Botanic Cottage
Royal Botanic Garden
John Adam 1766; Simpson & Brown Architects 2016

The RBGE is rooted in a medicinal garden founded in 1670 near Holyrood Abbey. In 1676, it was moved to the grounds of Trinity College Kirk, and to Leith Walk in 1763 where a cottage was built for the head gardener. The cottage was left behind in the 1820s when the Botanics relocated to Inverleith. Much altered and reduced in size over the years, it was spared demolition, dismantled in 2008 and re-erected here in 2016. During the Scottish Enlightenment, medical students were taught botany in a classroom in the cottage. It has resumed its educational role, the centrepiece in the Botanics' Demonstration Garden.

147
Front Range Glasshouses
Royal Botanic Garden

Allan Pendreigh, George Pearce & John Johnson, Ministry of Public Building & Works Scotland 1964–7

Spectacular structure of high tensile steel and cable-stayed outriggers from

which the glass roof is suspended. It replaced a rusting range of Edwardian glasshouses. The design evolved from curator Dr EE Kemp's brief – to eliminate corrosion-prone internal support in the hot-house and maximise natural light and space for plants. To convince sceptics of the design's structural integrity, a full-scale mock-up was tested to destruction. Pure engineering, anticipating the High Tech style of a decade later.

148
Temperate Palm House
Royal Botanic Garden

Robert Matheson 1858; restored Simpson & Brown Architects 2002

Neoclassical sandstone façades and an iron and glass roof supported on cast iron columns, a typical 19th-century fusion of historicism and engineering. Behind the Temperate House is the garden's oldest glasshouse, the iron- and glass-domed Tropical Palm House (1834). It was the largest glasshouse in Britain at the time (the Temperate Palm House is the tallest of its type).

Both, along with the Front Range Glasshouses, are to be refurbished as part of the Edinburgh Biomes project, 'the most significant in the garden's history'. Its purpose is to maintain the Botanics' status as an international centre of plant research and biodiversity in the era of climate change. There will be several new buildings. Their architects face a perennial, very Edinburgh challenge – to acknowledge outstanding architectural heritage while building well for the future.

149
Modern Alpine House
Royal Botanic Garden

Smith Scott Mullan Associates 2013
Open-sided steel and glass pavilion with a dramatic roofscape like alpine scenery. The structure, which is 100 percent recy-
clable, creates a microclimate that limits the plants' exposure to rain while allowing natural light to penetrate and fresh air to circulate. The built form increases the wind speed below the roof to help simulate the dry mountain-top conditions that suit Alpine plants, which are displayed here in a naturalis-tic bedding of tufa, a porous rock.

In complete contrast to the delicate Alpine plants – a contrast typical of the extremes of scale and habitat to be found in the Botanics – are the giant redwoods in the John Muir Grove. The grove, formerly the Upper Woodland Garden, was renamed in 1990 to honour Dunbar, East Lothian-born John Muir, the Scottish-American explorer, environmentalist and writer whose work led to the foundation the US National Parks system.

The grove is in the south-east section of the garden, near East Gate Lodge (William Playfair 1826), now a visitor reception and café (Smith Scott Mullan Associates 2010). The architects also refurbished the RBGE's Victorian lecture theatre (2013) and designed the Plant Sales Glasshouse (2012) at John Hope Gateway.

150
Fettes College
Carrington Road, Inverleith

David Bryce 1864–70
William Fettes was a wine and tea merchant, a director of the British Linen Bank and twice Lord Provost. He died at his townhouse at 13 Charlotte

Square in 1836 leaving no heirs. His bequest funded this school 'for the education of children of reduced circumstances.' It was a charity, but like others of its origin it is now a bastion of private education. The building represents nothing but the best, both for the underprivileged for whom it was intended and the reputation of its benefactor.

The style is French Renaissance laced with 19th-century medievalism. There are Gothic pinnacles galore, Loire château-style conical turrets, faux-medieval statuary (John Rhind sculptor), and gargoyles, grape vines,

birds, serpents and bees. On the wide, gravel square is the school's evocative War Memorial (William Birnie Rhind) – a fallen Highland officer, flanked by a lion and stag, inspiring his men with the words 'Carry on'. The bronze figure, unveiled in 1921, turned out to have been flawed in casting and was replaced, recast in the original form (c. 1933).

Fettes is not open to the public. No matter, because Bryce's French fantasy is best seen from Fettes Avenue and Carrington Road. The iron gates display lion-and-stag heraldry with the motto 'Industria', symbolised by a bee derived from William Fettes' coat of arms. His mausoleum is in Canongate Kirkyard, in the Old Town where he started trading.

151
Spens Building
Fettes College

Page\Park Architects 2015

The wooded and landscaped Fettes campus has a variety of Victorian and Edwardian buildings and modern architecture. Among the former are the chapel attached to the main building, the headmaster's house, halls of residence and a cricket pavilion.

In 2004, Page\Park Architects devised a masterplan for future development and subsequently designed several buildings, notably the energy-efficient Spens Building, for art, music and other studies. Its built form is at once modern and traditional: stone cladding and gables contrast with glazed extrusions; ventilation shafts are expressed as chimneys, a counterpoint to

the thrusting vertical forms of Bryce's main building. Also of interest, on a slate-clad podium, is the mid-century modern Dining Hall (William Kininmonth 1967), glazed below a lead panelled wrap. The sculptural object at the entrance is the school Centenary Stone.

152
FetLor Youth Club
122 Crewe Road South

James Robertson Architect 2017

Founded in 1924 as Fettesian-Lorettonian Boys' Club to provide a 'hot meal and a bath for the poor boys' of the Old Town, and in memory of former pupils of Fettes and Loretto schools killed in the First World War and comrades-in-arms from the city's slums who also died.

The new clubhouse has an external pattern of Corten steel panels, which weather to form a protective layer. The entrance is behind a privacy screen, to create 'the sense that the members are in a fort, where they feel safe and protected.' There is a sports hall on the ground floor and multipurpose rooms upstairs, all accessed from the foyer's double-height atrium. Activities and studies help young people gain confidence and self-esteem. A stone's throw from Fettes, it shows that good contemporary architecture need not be exclusive to the privileged few.

153

MRC (Medical Research Council) Institute of Genetics and Molecular Medicine

Western General Hospital

Crew Road South

Oberlanders Architects 2016

The University of Edinburgh's IGMM links three existing buildings to form an integrated research centre for disease prevention, diagnosis and treatment. The new building, with a façade vertically finned as a solar screen, is energy-efficient, rated BREEAM Excellent. Spatial planning promotes multi-disciplinary collaboration; the atrium acts as a circulation and gathering space. The architects described their role modestly: 'facilitating people to do important good work.'

154

Nuffield Transplantation Surgery Unit

Hospital Main Drive

Peter Womersley 1965–8

Visually expressive bunker built to insulate a purpose-designed facility for transplant surgery, said to have been the world's first. The plan, with sterilisation unit, operating suite and patients' rooms, responded to the personal specification of pioneering surgeon Michael Woodruff.

The sculptural forms are characteristic of Brutalism (from the French *béton brut*, meaning 'raw concrete'). The architect was inspired by the material's aesthetic and engineering potential, here a combination of poured-in-place reinforced concrete and panels pre-cast off-site. Cantilevered beams carry floor and roof slabs. The main floor was cantilevered over the plant room on the sloping site. The ventilation tower has stairs to a skywalk that connects to other hospital services. The building has since been repurposed as the Western's chemotherapy centre. An extension (Aitken Turnbull Architects 2007) respects the original's scale and volume.

155

St Cuthbert's Poorhouse

Hospital Main Drive

Peddie & Kinnear 1867

Above the entrance is an eroded plaque: 'Erected by the Parochial Board of the Parish of St Cuthbert'; the date, architects and the board's chairman are also recorded. The previous facility, a charity workhouse and school for orphans run by St Cuthbert's Church, was demolished to make way for the Caledonian Railway station and hotel (see 121).

The new poorhouse, dressed in French Renaissance-style, was as up to date as the railway hotel, with steam boilers for central heating and constant hot water, but a world away in every other respect. The 400 or so inmates were segregated in sections for the 'Very Decent, Decent, Bastardy and Depraved' and no doubt treated accordingly. The building was requisitioned by the military in 1915 for wounded soldiers. It is now part of the Western General Hospital.

156

Maggie's Centre

The Stables, Hospital Main Drive

Richard Murphy Architects, Emma Keswick landscape design 1996

Nothing could be further from judgmental Victorian attitudes to health care than Maggie's Centres, of which this was the first. The centres, inspired by the late Maggie Jencks, provide counselling and comfort to those diagnosed with cancer, in settings that are inclusive and informal.

The initiative caught the attention of other prominent architects. The twenty-sixth centre in Britain opened in Leeds in 2020. Each has a unique personality. The original here is a sympathetic conversion of a 19th-century stable block. It was shortlisted for the Royal Institute of British Architects (RIBA) Stirling Prize 1997. Extended twice (Richard Murphy Architects 2001 and 2018).

McEwan Hall, the University of Edinburgh

The most opulent purpose built graduation and concert hall in Europe
and probably the only one funded by sales of beer. Its benefactor was
brewery baron William McEwan. The belle-époque auditorium is as grand
as any opera house. Neoclassical murals symbolising Arts and Sciences
adorn the dome. When the hall opened in 1897, McEwan was presented
with an honorary doctorate and the Freedom of the City.

The University of Edinburgh was established by the town council
in 1583. McEwan Hall is the most palatial building in its patrimony –
architecture of every period from the 17th to 20th centuries: from Moray
House, St Cecilia's Hall, the Old College and the Playfair Library to the
modernist library designed by Basil Spence.

4

The South Side

Old Medical School—Royal Infirmary Buildings—Quartermile—
Edinburgh Printmakers—King's Theatre—Barclay Viewforth
Church—Merchiston Castle—Dominion Cinema—Reid Memorial
Church—Hermitage of Braid—Royal Observatory—Royal Common-
wealth Pool—National Library of Scotland—St Peter's Episcopal
Church—Summerhall—George Square—University of Edinburgh
Library—Potterrow—McEwan Hall . . .

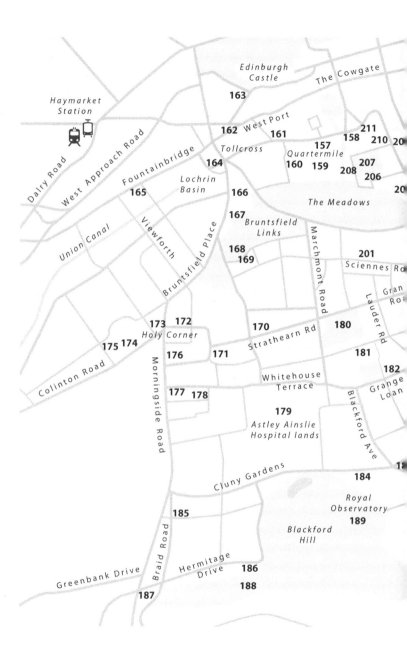

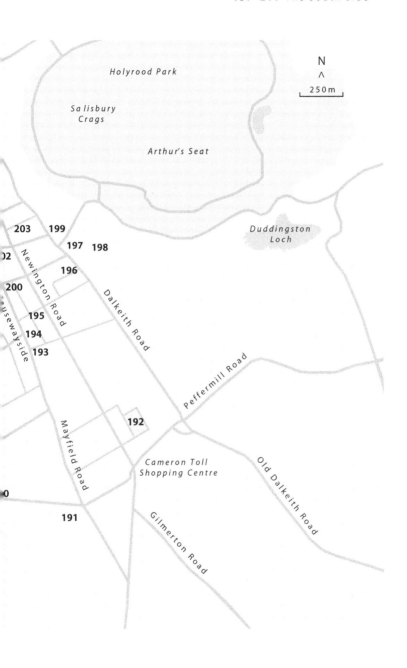

Holyrood Park

Salisbury
Crags

Arthur's Seat

Duddingston
Loch

N
∧
250m

203 **199**

197 **198**

02

196

200

195

194

193

192

191

Newington Road

Causewayside

Dalkeith Road

Peffermill Road

Mayfield Road

Cameron Toll
Shopping Centre

Old Dalkeith Road

Gilmerton Road

0

157
Royal Infirmary Buildings
Lauriston Place
David Bryce 1870–9

Sprawling complex laid out with parallel blocks isolated to reduce the possibility of infections spreading (an innovation at the time). Its Old Surgical Building is a tour de force of Scots Baronial style. Above the entrance is a plaque with the dates 1729 and 1870: the former the birth of the original infirmary at High School Yards; the latter this building's foundation. There are biblical inscriptions: 'I was a stranger and ye took me in; I was sick and ye visited me'; and in Latin, *Ad Sanitatem Gentium. Patet Omnibus*, meaning 'Towards the health of the nation. Open to everyone.' The words recall Lord Provost George Drummond, whose idea the original infirmary, for rich and poor alike, was.

The site was sold in 2001. The Royal Infirmary moved to Little France. The buildings are now part of Quartermile, for which the Old Surgical Building was to have been a hotel. In 2017, it was bought by the University of Edinburgh to be retrofitted as the Edinburgh Futures Institute (Bennetts Associates architects). Across Lauriston Place is George Heriot's School (see 43).

158
Old Medical School
The University of Edinburgh
Teviot Place
Robert Rowand Anderson 1876–86
The Faculty of Medicine, modelled on the medical schools at Padua and

Leiden, was established in 1726. It is the oldest in Britain. It was located at High School Yards in the Old Town. By the mid 19th century, more space was needed, for which a competition was announced in 1874.

Anderson was one of six architects invited to compete. He won the commission after making 'a whirlwind study tour of medical schools and lecture theatres in England, France, Holland and Germany'. His Venetian Renaissance design had a *campanile* and a graduation hall. The tower was not built here (see 125) but the hall was, eventually (211). The barrel-vaulted entrance to the school leads to an inner courtyard, the Anatomical Museum (established in 1884 as a teaching resource) and the classic Lecture Theatre.

159
Quartermile
Lauriston Place

Foster + Partners architects, Arup engineers; constructed 2005–19

Described by Foster + Partners as 'one of the largest and most comprehensive regeneration schemes in Scotland.' Their masterplan (2003) featured housing, offices, a hotel, restaurants, cafés and shops. It was rolled out on the old Royal Infirmary site, which overlooks the Meadows (the historic park on land reclaimed from Burgh Loch in the 17th and 18th centuries).

The plan considered the hospital's Victorian buildings, with their embedded carbon footprint, as sustainable assets. In any event, heritage listing required they be retained. The former nursing wards have been retrofitted as flats (CDA Group architects, Will Rudd Davidson engineers). Modern apartment blocks are aligned for views of the park and scaled to fit between the old buildings. A Miesian aesthetic was applied to new construction; landscape design too is modernist, restrained. The project survived the financial crash of 2008. In 2013, it was marketed in Hong Kong and Singapore, a first for an Edinburgh development – globalisation, slick and stylish. Public space feels private, but the urban design is respectful of the setting which is within Edinburgh's World Heritage Site.

160

Wharton Square

Chalmers Street

Richard Murphy Architects, Arup
engineers 2013

Massive Euro-style block, with an inner
courtyard thoughtfully planned to max-
imise daylight to all flats. Its scale owes much to the monumental courtyard
blocks of social housing in 1920s Vienna, an influence the architects acknowledge. Built for Quartermile & Hillcrest Housing Association. Dazzle cladding
outrageous and enjoyable.

161

**The Fire Station, Edinburgh College
of Art**

Lauriston Place

Robert Morham, City Architect 1900

Edinburgh was the world's first munici-
pality with a regular fire service, formed
when the Great Fire of 1824 destroyed part of the Old Town. The founder
was James Braidwood, the first Master of Fire Engines; his motto, 'Aye Ready'
(there is a plaque here in his honour; also a statue on Parliament Square). This
was the Central Fire Station until operations were transferred to Tollcross (see
164). Fire trucks (originally horse-drawn) were garaged in the Engine Room
(it became a fire service museum after Tollcross opened). There were living
quarters for the Firemaster and crews. An Edwardian baroque-style hose
tower was built at the rear.

In 2017, the fire station was bought by the University of Edinburgh to
expand Edinburgh College of Art – a Beaux-Arts *palais* (JM Dick Peddie 1909;
upgraded LDN Architects 2018). Its sculpture court displays the Parthenon
Frieze, plaster casts from moulds made in Athens by the Earl of Elgin (see 71).

162

St Cuthbert's Co-operative Society Buildings

Bread Street

Parisian domed corner (Thomas Waller Marwick 1914), originally St Cuthbert's

Emporium, part of the co-op's Bread Street complex. Rehabilitated as a hotel, 'The Point' (Andrew Doolan c. 1996), now a Hilton. Next door is the former drapery store (John McLachlan 1892), and next to that the most progressive piece of architecture the co-op built – the furniture showroom, with the first glazed curtain wall in Scotland (David Harvey, Philip McManus, Thomas Waller Marwick 1937). Interior gone, but when the façade was renovated as part of the hotel (Andrew Doolan c. 2000), the 1930s lettering style was revived to spell 'Conference Centre'.

163
Castle Terrace
James Gowans 1866–70

Unique tenement block composed with restless invention and fanciful features. There are domes like crowns, massed ranks of chimneys, hooded eaves and gables, and spandrels with Moorish serrated stonework. The corner gable has *putti* representing a mason and an architect; above them is an unidentified Greek or Roman goddess (William Brodie sculptor). Gowans also designed houses, two of them very strange (see 175).

164
Tollcross Community Fire Station
Ponton Street, West Tollcross
Lothian Regional Council (architects)

Scottish Fire and Rescue Service fire hall built in 1986 as a regional control and training centre to replace the old Central Fire Station (see 161). The exterior is a collision of postmodern forms trendy at the time. The artwork attached was commissioned by competition, to celebrate firefighters' courage and dedication to duty. An Edinburgh College of Art students' project produced the winning design (David Roxburgh artist).

165

Edinburgh Printmakers

Castle Mills, 1 Dundee Street, Fountainbridge

1894; Page\Park Architects, Will Rudd Davidson engineers 2018

Built as the head office of the North British Rubber Company, established in 1856 by two Americans who arrived in Scotland with a Goodyear patent. They bought and converted Castle Silk Mills on the north side of the Union Canal, a 19th-century transport asset now recreational. Castle Mills became the city's largest industrial enterprise, employing 3,000 people. They made rubber products, notably Wellington boots – more than one million pairs of boots for troops in the trenches of the First World War. The factory closed in the 1970s. The site was redeveloped for Fountainbridge Brewery, also gone.

This is the only North British Rubber Co. building left. It was saved from decay by Edinburgh Printmakers and retrofitted with spaces for printmaking and the visual arts, exhibitions, offices, a shop and café. The industrial patina was preserved as part of the continuing narrative of the historic site. The new entrance on Dundee Street has gates with a design symbolising sheet rubber production rollers and, by happenstance, printmaking (Rachel Duckhouse artist). Many heritage features were retained – cast iron columns, brick walls, timber trusses, skylights and the original doorway, entrance hall and staircase. The project has won several awards, including the Edinburgh Architectural Association (EAA) Building of the Year 2020.

166

King's Theatre

2 Leven Street

John Daniel Swanston & James Davidson 1906

Edwardian baroque façade with a curved pediment, paired columns and, at cornice level, the theatrical masks Comedy and Tragedy. Andrew Carnegie laid the foundation stone. The internal structure

is concrete and steel, with cantilevered balconies. The first show was *Cinderella*.

The auditorium is flamboyant with rococo plasterwork. Refurbishment (Smith Scott Mullan Associates, Will Rudd Davidson engineers) included a ceiling mural, *All the World's a Stage*, by artist and playwright John Byrne. It was unveiled in 2013 for the Edinburgh Festival, the creative spirit of which it conveys. The mural is one of the few visible changes since Edwardian times. A comprehensive upgrade is planned (Bennetts Associates architects). Next door (8 Leven Street) is Bennets Bar (1839). The décor (1906) is amazing – one of the finest traditional pub interiors in Edinburgh.

167
Barclay Viewforth Church
1 Wright's Houses
Frederick Thomas Pilkington 1864

Bizarre masterpiece beside the historic golf course, Bruntsfield Links. It was built for the Free Church of Scotland following a bequest and a competition won by Pilkington, a 'rogue architect' with a taste for Ruskinian Gothic style. The stonework is variegated in the Venetian manner. There are ghost stones, as if the masons stopped work yesterday. Carvings on the west side – palm fronds, grape vines and the biblical shepherd with sheep – show how elaborate (and costly) the sculptural scheme intended was.

Stone angels hover at the doorway. The interior is a theatrical space, with galleries and a timber roof (stencilled decoration and organ case by Sydney Mitchell). The plan is an ingenious response to the tight site. Dream-like spooky roofscape and spiky spire – at 76 metres the tallest in the city until St Mary's Cathedral was built (see 130). A roost for crows or a dragon's lair perhaps. Edinburgh architecture on the wild side.

168
Old Boroughmuir School
Warrender Park Crescent
John Alexander Carfrae 1904
Designed in Northern Renaissance style with baroque touch-
es for Boroughmuir School. It
became James Gillespie's High
School in 1914 after Boroughmuir relocated to 26 Viewforth, also by Carfrae,
now flats (2020). Novelist Muriel Spark, a pupil at Gillespie's from 1923 to
1935, recalled 'large classrooms, and big windows that looked out over the
leafy trees, the skies, and the swooping gulls of Bruntsfield Links.' Her classic novel, *The Prime of Miss Jean Brodie*, was inspired by her time here. The
building is now student accommodation for the University of Edinburgh.
Gillespie's campus is at 120 Warrender Park Road. New Boroughmuir School
(Allan Murray Architects 2018) is at 111 Viewforth, by the Union Canal.

169
Warrender Park Crescent
W & D Macgregor builders c. 1880
Bourgeois tenements abound in this suburb built
(1870–1914) after the feuing of the Warrender family's Marchmont estate. The plan, with streetscapes
of Scots Baronial-style tenements, was drawn in
1869 by architect David Bryce. The more ornate
blocks were designed by architects; others, like
the four-storey walk-ups shown here, were by builders using stock plans. The
only building here actually designed by Bryce is the three-storey 2–4 Alvan-
ley Terrace (1870) on Whitehouse Loan.

Marchmont and neighbouring Bruntsfield are high-density, walkable
Victorian neighbourhoods, case studies for sustainable urban design today.

170
Gillis Centre
Whitehouse Loan and Strathearn Road
The administrative centre of the Archdiocese of St Andrews and Edinburgh,

named after Bishop James Gillis who founded St Margaret's Convent (1834), the first in Scotland since the Reformation. Architect James Gillespie Graham designed the buildings, including a Romanesque-style chapel. In 1846, the chapel was altered with Gothic additions by Augustus Welby Pugin; his son, EW Pugin, designed the Gothic Revival school (1863).

171
St Bennets Chapel
42 Greenhill Gardens

> *John Henderson (villa c. 1859); Robert Weir Schultz (chapel) 1907*

Hard to find a more incongruous sight in Morningside than this Byzantine chapel in the garden of a 17th-century-style Victorian villa. The house was built for advocate George Seaton. It was bought In 1890 by the Archdiocese of St Andrews and Edinburgh as the archbishop's residence, for which a chapel was required. The chapel's benefactor was the 3rd Marquess of Bute, with whom architect Schultz, a Scottish Arts and Crafts designer, was associated. Schultz had studied Byzantine architecture in Greece, which might explain the form here: Greek cross in plan, Byzantine dome. Interior reportedly Italianate, with modern stained glass by Gabriel Loire of Chartres (1969).

172
John Livingstone Memorial Stone
1 Chamberlain Road

A gateway with a 17th-century scroll leads to a stone walled enclosure. Inside is a memorial stone inscribed *Mors Patet Hora Latet,* meaning 'Death is sure, the hour uncertain.' Illustrating this grim epigram is a winged hour glass, a skull and cross bones and a eulogy dated 1645, the year of the Great Plague. The eulogy ends: 'No age shall loose his memory.' The victim is thought to be John Livingstone, laird of the lands of Greenhill, by the Borough Muir, but no memory of him survives. The muir, part of which survives as Bruntsfield Links, was where the plague-afflicted were banished from the city for isolation and burial in unmarked graves.

173

Christ Church Morningside

6a Morningside Road

Hippolyte Blanc 1876

French Gothic style, busy with flying buttresses on the apse beside the tower and soaring spire. Built for the Scottish Episcopal Church, it is one of four churches at 'Holy Corner', the crossroads where Bruntsfield and Morningside meet. The others are Morningside Baptist Church (1874), Morningside United Church (1929) and North Morningside Parish Church (1879).

The Romanesque-style North Morningside Church is now the Eric Liddell Centre, a charity for which the interior was cleverly converted, creating a building within a building (Groves-Raines Architects 1994). Heritage features, notably stained glass windows, were retained. It is named after local hero, Olympic athlete and missionary Eric Liddell.

174

Merchiston Castle

Edinburgh Napier University

10 Colinton Road

Fifteenth-century tower house built by the Napiers of Merchiston. It was besieged in 1572 by forces loyal to Mary Queen of Scots during the civil war of the time (a cannonball was later found embedded below the battlements). The curious door in midair was probably accessed from a drawbridge on a platform in the courtyard. The castle would have been protected by an outer defensive wall. The arched gateway with carved lions and rusticated banded pillars on Colinton Road is a mystery from the 18th-century: its provenance is not known.

Merchiston Castle School, founded in 1828, was here until relocated to Colinton in 1930. The city bought the castle in 1935, but it was not occupied until the 1960s when it was restored (Stuart Harris architect) and incorporated into Napier Technical College (Alison & Hutchison & Partners 1961–4). The college, named after theologian, inventor and mathematician John Napier, once resident here, is now Edinburgh Napier University.

175

'Lammerburn'

10 Napier Road

James Gowans 1860

Gowans studied building design while working in his father's quarrying, construction and
railway-building company, which he took over in 1849. His architecture was
consistently eccentric. In 1885, he was appointed Edinburgh's Dean of Guild.
He promoted the International Exhibition of Industry, Science and Art held
on the Meadows in 1886, for which he designed the lion and unicorn Masons'
Memorial Pillars (they were intended to test different types of quarried stone
for durability; they still stand, at the west end of Melville Drive). He received a
knighthood but was declared bankrupt in 1888.

As Dean of Guild he was responsible for building regulations but, perhaps
fortunately for Edinburgh, not style. He built the city's scariest villa, Rockville
(1858), a 'Chinese Gothic pagoda' neighbours called 'Nightmare Abbey',
which stood across the road from Lammerburn. His financial woes forced its
sale. It survived until 1966, when it was demolished despite a campaign to
save it. Only the gateposts and boundary wall remain. A sculpture from the
garden, 'The Genius of Architecture' (William Brodie 1862), was re-erected in
West Princes Street Gardens, where it can be seen today.

Lammerburn is strange too, like Rockville but less alarming, built with
stones cut to a modular pattern, a Gowans innovation. He also designed his
own tombstone, erected in Grange Cemetery (see 180).

176

Church Hill Theatre

33 Morningside Road

Hippolyte Blanc 1892

Former Morningside Free Church. Palladian
style with a Roman Doric-columned porch,
Venetian window and pediment with oculus and garlands. Repurposed as a
theatre (1962–5) for amateur music and drama. City-owned, managed by the
Assembly Rooms (see 107). In the forecourt are the Church Hill Milestones
(Kenny Munro sculptor 1996), two pillars decorated with references to local
history and people.

177

Dominion Cinema

18 Newbattle Terrace

Thomas Bowhill Gibson 1938

'Morningside's favourite family-owned cinema', founded by cinephile Captain WM Cameron. Architect Gibson designed several cinemas of which this is the star – Moderne style with a vertical fin for signage and horizontal marquee, but no Hollywood Art Deco detailing, perhaps to cut costs. Retrofitted as a bijou multi-screen venue.

178

St Peter's Church Morningside

77 Falcon Avenue

Robert Lorimer 1907, Lorimer & Matthew 1929

Italianate, as if from a Renaissance painting. The client was Father John Gray who studied for the priesthood at the Scots College in Rome. The *campanile* stands above a courtyard. Romanesque nave completed in 1929. An angel in a niche outside holds a model of the clergy house, the first part of the two-stage build.

179

Charles Bell Pavilion

Astley Ainslie Hospital

Whitehouse Terrace (Grange Loan)

Michael Laird & Partners 1965

Modernist block poised above the ground in the manner of Le Corbusier. It was the first rehabilitation unit in Britain for convalescing children. Outside, there is therapeutic parkland with meadows, mature trees and wildlife. The pavilion and its setting illustrate the opinion expressed in a 1944 manifesto, *Building Scotland*, that 'brightness, freshness and good planning on an open site' are essential qualities for healthcare architecture.

The hospital was established by the bequest in 1900 of farmer David

Ainslie in memory of his nephew, John Astley Ainslie, who died young. Trustees bought the property here in 1920. The hospital, which opened in 1923, pioneered occupational therapy in Scotland. It is set to close. In 2020, the Astley Ainslie Community Trust commissioned from Oliver Chapman Architects a feasibility study for community ownership of the site.

Lost somewhere in the landscape is St Roque Chapel (1504; demolished c. 1800), named for the French patron saint of plague victims. Many were brought here from the Old Town for quarantine, the dead buried in mass graves. St Roque lives on in the name of a Victorian villa bought for the hospital in 1945. Ecclesiastical stones set in a low wall in the north-west section of the grounds were thought to be relics of St. Roque Chapel, but more likely were salvaged from Trinity College Kirk (see 19).

180
Grange Cemetery
Grange and Beaufort Roads
Laid out by architect David Bryce in 1847, with leafy avenues and a ridge of spooky catacombs. On the cemetery's north wall is a memorial in Egyptian style: a palm tree as an oasis of rest; a niche leading to the afterlife; a broken column for lives cut short. It was made for William Stuart of J & W Stuart, fishing net makers of Musselburgh. Also here, the tomb of architect James Gowans, like a detail from one of his buildings. The pyramid shape suggests freemasonry. Gowans and Stuart were probably members of the fraternity.

181
Grange Park House
38 Dick Place
Frederick Thomas Pilkington 1864–70
Eccentric villa with Romanesque features, originally the architect's home, now flats. It can be seen from Calton Cricket Ground on Grange Loan; its pretty gate lodge (1875) with bargeboard trim is on Dick Place. Numbers 48 and 50 Dick Place (c. 1863) are also unconventional by Pilkington. The Lane House at 46a Dick Place

(Kininmonth & Spence 1933), a modernist design which probably shocked the neighbours, was the home of architect William Kininmonth.

182
Grange House Wyverns
Grange Loan

Two Victorian gateposts, each bearing a wyvern (a heraldic winged serpent). The wyverns guarded the carriage drive of Grange House (not to be confused with Grange Park House). It was an ancient tower house given a baronial makeover in the 19th century, demolished in 1936 and the property subdivided for bungalows. The wyverns were relocated: this one is at the south foot of Lovers' Loan; the other is near where Lauder Road meets Grange Loan, the south-east boundary of the former estate.

183
Reid Memorial Church
West Savile Terrace at Blackford Avenue

Leslie Grahame Thomson 1929–33

Built in memory of William Reid 'in accordance with his last wish' for the congregation displaced from its place of worship on The Mound, which was required for New College library.

Architect Thomson commissioned renderings from Basil Spence to show how the new church would look – stunning in Spence's drawings and reality. The tower and lantern are offset from the cruciform plan (barrel-vaulted nave, chancel and short transepts). Decoration recalls Arts and Crafts style. A painted altarpiece illustrates The Last Supper. The Resurrection is a forceful theme, expressed in the building's vertical forms. The apse, which soars with a monumental trio of stained glass windows depicting the Nativity, Crucifixion and Ascension (designed by James Ballantine), steps into a quiet cloister where there is a biblical bas-relief by Alexander Carrick.

184
Sillitto House
32 Charterhall Road
Morris & Steedman 1960

Mid-century modern house on rising ground, now surrounded by a suburb of conventional homes. The first owners, Dick and Winifred Sillitto, were advised by a building society manager that what they needed was 'a nice little bungalow in Corstorphine'. Instead they hired Morris & Steedman after seeing, in 1958, an exhibition of work by young Scottish architects at the '57 Gallery.

The upper floor is a timber-framed box, glazed for natural light and views; the sides are timber-clad. The ground floor's concrete blocks were 'lime-washed like a typical Scottish country cottage'. The 'upside-down house' – bedrooms are downstairs and the kitchen and living spaces in the open-plan box above – still gleams with modernist clarity.

185
South Morningside Church
15 Braid Road
Robert Rowand Anderson 1892
Gothic Revival landmark with a herringbone-patterned needle spire and an octagonal stair with lantern attached to the tower. In 1974, the congregation merged with Morningside Parish Church (Hippolyte Blanc 1890) down the road. South Morningside became the parish community centre (closed in 2016).

One block uphill, in the middle of the road, are the Braid Stones where, in the winter of 1815, gallows were raised to execute two highwaymen. The judge directed they be punished, not at the Tolbooth jail in the Old Town, but at the scene of the crime, to where they were made to walk in the snow, followed by a crowd of spectators. The 'Hanging Stanes' mark the last executions in Scotland for highway robbery.

186

Ball House

28 Hermitage Drive

Hoskins Architects, David Narro
Associates engineers 2013

Carbon-neutral house sustained by photovoltaic cells and a biomass boiler. From a distance it looks agricultural, on the edge of Blackford Hill Local Nature Reserve. The structure is steel-framed on reinforced concrete, clad with timber siding and stone panels. Its angular forms contrast rather than clash with neighbouring stone-built homes, to which its scale is sympathetic; for example 'Shieldaig', 24 Hermitage Drive, an Arts and Crafts villa (Robert Lorimer 1907).

187

Greenbank Parish Church Extension

Braidburn Terrace at Comiston Road

Lee Boyd Architects 2001

Multipurpose steel-framed facility clad in western red cedar on a steeply sloping site. The shift from old to new is clear and the internal spatial planning, over three levels, clever. The church building (Alexander Lorne Campbell 1927) is reinforced concrete, clad in neo-Gothic stonework pierced by stained glass windows (James Ballantine, Alexander Strachan, William Wilson artists, 1928 to 1957). Next door is the original parish church (1900), now the Main Hall, an events space.

188

Hermitage of Braid

69a Braid Road

Robert Burn 1785

Enter at the Lodge Coffee House (1888), originally a tollhouse at 259 Morningside Road (the number can be spotted on one of its lintels). Walk down into the wooded glen where Braid burn burbles. On its north side is a doocot like some medieval relic (but of no great age). Follow the burn to a sudden meadow where the Hermitage appears as if from a fairy tale, eccentric with Palladian windows, a Georgian fanlight, bartizans and a machiolated parapet.

The name is thought to refer to a hermit here in the 17th century. The first known owner of the lands was Henri de Brad, son of a 12th-century Flemish knight. In 1772, nobleman Charles Gordon of Cluny bought the Braid estate and built the Hermitage. The house and grounds were gifted to the city by John McDougal, a Leith grain merchant, and opened to the public in 1938. Deer and wild boar were once hunted in the forest, now Blackford Hill Local Nature Reserve.

189
The Royal Observatory
Blackford Hill
Walter Wood Robertson, HM Office of Works 1894
The facility was moved from Calton Hill to Blackford Hill where there was space for a state-of-the-art building on a site with clear views of the night sky, far away from Auld Reekie's light pollution and smog. The architectural style is Italianate. There are two octagonal towers (the taller one shown here). Each supports a metal-framed, copper-clad drum designed to house telescopes which can be pointed at any chosen star. Each drum has a delicately patterned halo of Greek decoration.

Based here are the UK Astronomy Technology Centre and the University of Edinburgh's Institute for Astronomy. The library houses the Crawford Collection of astronomical books and manuscripts, donated along with optical instruments by James Ludovic Lindsay, 26th Earl of Crawford, patron of the observatory.

190
Harrison Memorial Arch
Observatory Road
Sydney Mitchell 1888
A triumphal arch, not, as might be supposed, the gate to the Royal Observatory but a

monument to Lord Provost George Harrison praising his life 'devoted to the public good'. A plaque records that during his time in office Blackford Hill was acquired and opened as a public park, in 1884. A bronze portrait of him is set in the pediment.

191

King's Buildings, The University of Edinburgh
West Mains Road
Lorimer & Matthew 1924–31

The campus was named after King George V who laid the foundation stone of the Joseph Black (Chemistry) Building (A F Balfour Paul) in 1920. Other buildings followed as faculties relocated from the Old Town.

The Zoology Building contains the university's natural history collection, begun the 17th century at the Old College. On the façades are zoological medallions with creatures from the sub-Arctic, tropical Africa, the Orient, Oceania and South America (Phyllis Bone sculptor). The Geology Build-ing (the Grant Institute) houses the Cockburn Geological Museum. Above the entrance is a figure studying a fossil, sculpted with characteristic vigour by Alexander Carrick. The Engineering Building also has a symbolic figure by Carrick, on top of its Art Deco entrance bay. Bone and Carrick brought artistic prestige to the architecture here, having worked with Robert Lorimer at the

National War Memo-rial (see 52).

Award-winning recent buildings on campus include Arcadia Nursery, a

cross-laminated timber structure (Malcolm Fraser Architects 2014), and the box-shaped Noreen and Kenneth Murray Library (Austin-Smith: Lord 2012). Both are highly sustainable, energy-efficient and rated BREEAM Excellent. Also future-focused is FloWave Ocean Energy Research Facility (Bennetts Associates architects, Arup engineers 2014). Looks like a warehouse, but inside is one of the world's most advanced research facilities for wave and tidal renewable technology.

192
Suffolk Halls of Residence
East Suffolk Park
Robertson & Swan 1913–17; 1925–8

The buildings here were the first purpose built halls of residence for female students in Scotland. There are five blocks, built for the University of Edinburgh in two phases around a 'village green', a step back in time. They look like Franco-Scottish country houses of the 17th century but are essentially Edwardian, influenced by the Arts and Crafts architecture of Robert Lorimer.

193
Mayfield Salisbury Parish Church
West Mayfield and Mayfield Road
Hippolyte Blanc 1879

Originally Mayfield Free Church, founded in 1875 to serve the growing suburb of Newington. Hippolyte Blanc was appointed architect after winning a design competition with this characteristic French Gothic sermon. The tower and steeple were added in 1895. The long, barrel-vaulted plaster roof (David Carr and Stewart Tod 1970) is a simplified simulation of the original timber structure which was destroyed by fire in 1969. The rest of the church was spared, including its superb collection of stained glass windows.

194
Leslie's Bar
45–47 Ratcliffe Terrace
Peter Henderson 1896
Architect Henderson's specialty was ornate
pub interiors. This is one of the best. Original
features include Adamesque friezes, plasterwork cornices and ceiling roses,
timber gantry and clock, and a mahogany island bar with a screen on one
side said to have been for the privacy of posh patrons. Frontage with Ionic
pilasters also original. The bar occupies the ground floor of a tenement, a
typical urban and social arrangement. John Leslie was an early licensee.

195
Bartholomew House
12 Duncan Street
Cousin, Ormiston & Taylor 1911
Former head office, studios and print works of
the Edinburgh Geographical Institute, better
known as John Bartholomew & Son, map engravers and publishers. It was
built by John George Bartholomew, fourth generation in a line of mapmakers
from 1797 and a founder of the Royal Scottish Geographical Society.

The portico and entrance hall were salvaged by Bartholomew from the
demolition in 1909 of Falcon Hall (1780), the family home. It was originally
called Morningside Lodge, built for a future Lord Provost. It was renamed by
Alexander Falconer, who bought it in 1814 having retired from the East India
Company. He commissioned architect Thomas Hamilton to add the portico,
and iron gates and stone pillars decorated with falcons. In 1874, the gates
and pillars were relocated to the gatehouse at Edinburgh Zoo and are still
there. Bartholomew House is now flats.

196
Arthur Lodge
Blacket Place at Dalkeith Road
Thomas Hamilton c. 1829
Attributed to Hamilton of Royal High School
fame, his Greek Revival style here downsized to

domestic scale. Porch and pediment composed to bring height and depth to the front elevation. Original gateway and carriage drive still in use. The villa was designed for Robert Mason, a builder who went bankrupt in 1830. It was bought by City Treasurer, David Cunningham (who had hired Hamilton for the Royal High School). Originally called 'Salisbury Cottage', Salisbury Crags being nearby, as is Arthur's Seat, hence 'Arthur Lodge'; or this might refer to Major James Arthur who bought the house in 1841. A subsequent owner was Andrew Usher (see 123).

Arthur Lodge stands on the east edge of the Blacket Estate, Edinburgh's first garden suburb, developed in the 1820s to a plan by architect James Gillespie Graham. The architecture is a mix of attractive Georgian and Victorian terraces and villas. Gate pillars to the estate can be seen on Dalkeith Road. The gates were closed at night to keep the riffraff out.

197
Royal Commonwealth Pool
21 Dalkeith Road

Robert Matthew, Johnson-Marshall & Partners (RMJM), Arup engineers 1967–70; S & P Architects, Buro Happold engineers, Graham Construction 2009–12

This spectacular city-owned aquatic centre was built for the 1970 Commonwealth Games. The event returned to Edinburgh in 1986 (also the diving competitions during the 2014 Commonwealth Games hosted by Glasgow). The seemingly shallow, horizontal modernist form is deceptive – inside is a luminous, virtually column-free space of considerable depth, truly epic in scale. A prodigious programme to renew the venue included the engineering challenge of constructing new pools without damaging the Grade-A heritage listed building's envelope. The comprehensive upgrade was completed in 2012.

198

Holland House and South Hall

Pollock Halls of Residence

18 Holyrood Park Road

Rowand Anderson, Kininmonth
& Paul 1952

Two courtyard blocks in cloistered, landscaped quadrangles bisected by an avenue leading to a dining hall. The architecture is modernist, of 1930s vintage despite the completion date. Clean-cut, Scandinavian with Swedish-inspired lanterns, a contrast to three Victorian baronial mansions, now part of the University of Edinburgh's estate here, built for book publisher Thomas Nelson and family.

199

Scottish Widows Building

15 Dalkeith Road

Basil Spence, Glover & Ferguson;
Arup engineers, Sylvia Crowe
landscape design 1972–6

Glass-walled reinforced concrete structure, partly on *pilotis* over a landscaped water feature. There are 12 interlocking, open-plan pods around two service cores. The hexagonal shape of the pods was inspired by the geological structure of basalt, the local volcanic rock. To preserve views of Arthur's Seat and Holyrood Park the complex was kept low. It seems to hover, like a space station about to land.

200

National Library of Scotland, Causewayside Building

33 Salisbury Place

Andrew Merrylees
Associates 1988; 1994

Stone-clad pinnacles and glazed stair towers with a grid pattern likened to the lattice forms of Charles Rennie Mackintosh. This is a beguiling connection but the window grid, internal partitions and floor panels were based the 90-cm module designed for the library's bookshelves. Service areas and circulation are oriented around the daylit perimeter, freeing the core, which extends two and a half floors below ground, for books and extensive collections of maps and marine charts. Stored here is the Bartholomew Archive (see 195).

201
Royal Hospital for Sick Children
9 Sciennes Road
George Washington Browne 1895
The hospital was founded in 1860, the first in Scotland specially for children. Its building near Lauriston Place was demolished after an outbreak of typhoid in 1890 and the site sold to the Royal Infirmary. Washington Browne's building is Northern Renaissance style with Flemish gables and a baroque doorway. Its Mortuary Chapel is decorated with murals (Phoebe Traquair 1886), salvaged from the typhoid-struck building and installed here in 1894. A new hospital for children has been built at the Royal Infirmary complex, Little France. Plans for residential conversion of the old one were approved in 2019. Ideally, the murals should be kept in situ and be accessible.

Next door is Sciennes Primary School, opened in 1892. Jacobean style by Robert Wilson, architect for the Edinburgh School Board.

202
Southern Motors Filling Station
39 Causewayside
Basil Spence 1933
Structurally expressive steel-framed and concrete garage in Moderne style with vertical fins for signage. Glazing is modernist, continental, Bauhaus-inspired. Offices were cantilevered above the forecourt where fuel was dispensed. A different liquid now: the building is a wine store.

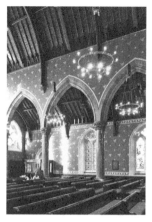

203
St Peter's Episcopal Church
14 Lutton Place
William Slater 1857–65
Medieval style praised in the Builder magazine as 'the most complete Gothic church in Edinburgh.' There are stained glass windows by Clayton & Bell, floor tiles by Minton and polished 'Scotch' granite pillars in the arcaded nave, where the walls and the timber roof were richly coloured with stencil work. Outside, the spire is patterned with cinquefoils. The narthex is cloister-like, to which is linked a serene and silent octagonal baptistry.

The statue of St Peter above the cavernous entrance was added in 1930s when, during a misguided 'modernisation', the original interior decoration was over-painted. In 2009, Benjamin Tindall Architects re-imagined and re-instated it, inspired by a Victorian engraving and physical evidence. A repeat pattern composed of St Peter's golden keys to heaven and a Celtic knot symbolising the Holy Trinity was applied to the re-coloured walls; fresh lighting evoking medieval ring chandeliers enhances the space. Gorgeous.

204
Summerhall Arts Complex
1 Summerhall Place
David McArthy 1916
This was the Royal (Dick) School of Veterinary Studies, founded in 1823 by veterinarian William Dick. In 2011, the Edwardian baroque building and neighbouring structures were revitalised as Summerhall, an A to Z of creative enterprises. The brutalist-style Techcube, previously the school's laboratory block (Alan Reiach, Eric Hall & Partners c. 1970), was repurposed with co-working spaces. There's a craft brewery too, in the court-yard behind the original building which was built on the site of Summerhall Brewery (1704), hence the old/new name.

205
Archers Hall
Buccleuch Street
Alexander Laing 1776; A F Balfour Paul
& Robert Rowand Anderson 1900

Home of the Royal Company of Archers, formed in 1676, the sovereign's ceremonial bodyguard in Scotland. The Venetian window and elaborate entrance date from 1900 when the 18th-century building was extended. Above the door is an armorial sculpture featuring archers and the motto in Latin, *Arcu atque animo,* meaning 'With bow and spirit'. There are new facilities for archery; also, low-rise flats for post-graduate students of the University of Edinburgh (LDN Architects 2011).

206
The University of Edinburgh Business School
29 Buccleuch Place
LDN Architects 2011

Jewel-like entrance pavilion, part of an upgrade to the Business School's Adam Ferguson Building (Robert Matthew, Johnson-Marshall & Partners c. 1966), one of several 1960s blocks once notorious for intruding on historic George Square. Rather than being replaced, they have been given energy-efficient, user-friendly makeovers – sustainable solutions for ageing assets.

207
George Square
James Brown 1766–85

Brown designed the square as a fashionable quarter of town-houses for the city's 'professional classes'. It preceded and probably influenced James Craig's plan for the New Town. The name refers to Brown's older brother, not King George. It was and remains the largest square in Edinburgh. Part of the north side was cleared in the 19th century for George Watson's Ladies College (the building now belongs to the University of Edinburgh). In the 1960s, the square was redeveloped to a modernist plan by Robert Matthew, the university's first Professor of Architecture. Only the west side (where Walter Scott was raised, at number 25), half of the east side and the gardens were spared.

Several monumental 'brutalist' buildings appeared: notably the 14-storey David Hume Tower (Robert Matthew Johnson-Marshall & Partners, Blyth & Blyth engineers 1960–3), named in honour of the eminent philosopher of the Scottish Enlightenment; the Lecture Theatre (same design team as the tower, 1965–70), a giant cantilevered box like a piece of Russian Constructivism; and the Main Library, a layered, almost geological slab (Basil Spence, Glover & Ferguson, Arup engineers 1965–7). They are now Grade A-listed by Historic Environment Scotland as exceptional examples of Scottish modernism, monuments to a time when architecture with visual and structural flair expressed faith in the future.

Heritage listing does not prevent buildings being renamed. In 2020, the University of Edinburgh, pending a review, cleansed the David Hume Tower of the philosopher's name, in response to research that revealed Hume condoned slavery and the white supremacist view of race. Scotland's leading historian, Tom Devine, condemned Hume's defenestration and found architectural comment irresistible: 'In History we teach our students not to indulge in the intellectual sin of anachronistic judgement; ie, never to

impose the values of today on those of the past . . . On the other hand, Hume might be relieved that the David Hume Tower, the ugliest modern building, among several on the central campus, no longer bears his name.'

208
Chapel of St Albert the Great
George Square Lane

Simpson & Brown Architects 2012

Hidden at the back of a townhouse (24 George Square) is this serene contempo-rary sacred space. The previous chapel, which the Dominican congregation had outgrown, was in a bay-windowed room of the house.

Quality of light was significant in the client's brief and is the new chapel's defining feature. Clerestory windows above sandstone walls illuminate the interior's envelope of stone and thinly striated oak. The roof above the altar is supported by a quartet of Corten steel columns which splay like the mature sycamore tree outside, connecting the space, through its glazed chancel, with nature in the garden. A green roof too, making the chapel, when seen from above, part of the landscape.

209
Central Mosque and Islamic Centre
50 Potterrow

Basil Al Bayati 1988–98

Islam meets Scots Baronial in this blend of eastern and western architectural forms. Towers with turrets look inspired by those at Holyrood Palace; the deep-set, arched entrances and minaret are authentic Islamic features.

The mosque is one of the largest in Scotland, with an immense prayer hall built to accommodate 1,200 worship-pers. The centre has a smaller hall for seminars and social events, a library, administration offices and a kitchen. Funding took some time, until King Fahd of Saudi Arabia contributed most of it. As in all mosques, the orienta-tion of the *mihrab* ensures worshippers pray facing Mecca.

210

Potterrow Development

The University of Edinburgh

Bennetts Associates architects, Buro Happold engineers 2005–8; 2016–18

Landmark complex on a site cleared in the 1960s between George and Bristo squares. The competition-winning entry (Bennetts Associates with Reiach & Hall Architects) was for one building, with construction phased. Bennetts Associates subsequently executed the whole project.

Essentially, there are three buildings – the Informatics Forum (computa-

tion, data processing) and the Dugald Stewart Building (philosophy, psychology and linguistics), both 2008, and the Bayes Centre (data technology, robotics), 2018. Complexity was rendered coherent with structural harmony and efficient spatial planning. Sandstone-clad, street-friendly forms reference the urban grain of the Old Town. The buildings enclose a courtyard that reinstates a historic pedestrian route between Bristo Square and Potterrow.

The complex was designed for human interaction, 'serendipity', as the architects put it. Circulation is focused around skylit atriums notable for exposed structural steelwork and helical white steel stairs. Most significant to the outcome was teamwork: the building programme had to resolve the needs of several research and educational clients. The first phase was a joint winner of the RIAS Andrew Doolan Award, Best Building in Scotland 2008.

211

McEwan Hall

The University of Edinburgh, Bristo Square

Robert Rowand Anderson 1887–97; LDN Architects, Buro Happold engineers 2014–17

Ceremonial graduation and concert hall gifted to the university by William

McEwan, founder in 1856 of the Fountain Brewery. Its most popular product was McEwan's Export, the beer of the British Empire.

The hall's design evolved from Anderson's scheme for the Medical School (see 158) which was built first; the hall ten years later due to lack of funding until McEwan intervened. It looks circular but is D-shaped in plan. The rhythmic Italianate exterior conceals a vast belle-époque auditorium. The centrepiece is a rare Hope-Jones concert organ in an enormous gilded oak, rococo case designed by Anderson. Above it, the dome is decorated with figurative murals (photo, pages 122–123) symbolising Arts and Sciences (William Palin artist).

In 2017, the hall reopened after a three-year refurbishment. A conspicuous new entrance was constructed – a circular pod complementing the curve of the 1890s façade. Downstairs in the pod is a short tunnel to the hall's circulation corridor in a brick-vaulted basement. A short ascent reveals the awe-inspiring auditorium.

McEwan Hall is now multipurpose. Its original function is seen in the tympanum above the old entrance, where there is a tableau of a graduation

ceremony. Also on the recently reconditioned Bristo Square are the ornamental McEwan Lantern Pillar (Robert Rowand Anderson c. 1890), presented to the city by the eponymous brewer; the Scots Baronial Teviot Row House (Sydney Mitchell & Wilson 1889), the world's oldest custom-built student union building (with twin, château-style stair towers modelled on those at the 16th-century Falkland Palace, Fife); and the neoclassical Reid Concert Hall (David Cousin 1858), originally the Reid School of Music.

The Shore, Leith Old Harbour

The scene seems almost Hanseatic, a reflection of Scotland's historic trade links with continental Europe. Exports included fish, coal, grain and animal hides; timber, wine, fruit and spices were notable imports. The formerly tidal haven, where the Water of Leith once flowed directly to the sea, is maintained at high-water level (a barrier and lock gate were installed in the outer harbour in 1968). Since the 1990s, the gritty Old Harbour has been gentrified.

The Port of Leith's prominence was eclipsed in the 19th century when Glasgow became Scotland's industrial, trading and shipbuilding capital. Leith still has the nation's largest enclosed deep-water harbour, with docks from where ships sail to service North Sea oil and gas fields and offshore wind farms. There is a cruise ship terminal and a unique visitor attraction, the Royal Yacht *Britannia*.

5

Newhaven, Leith & Portobello

Newhaven Harbour—Starbank House—Edinburgh Sculpture Workshop—Leith Fort—Ocean Terminal—North Leith Parish Church—Leith History Mural—St Ninian's Church—Cables Wynd House—Lamb's House—Leith Customs House—Merchant Navy Memorial—Leith Old Harbour—South Leith Parish Church—Trinity House—Craigentinny Marbles—St John the Evangelist Catholic Church—Portobello Swim Centre . . .

N
^
200m

Newhaven
Harbour
212

213

Main Street

Starbank
Park
214

Craighall Road

Hawthornvale
216

North Fort Street

217

East Trinity Road

215

Newhaven Road

Victoria Park

Ferry Road

< 240

Inchview
Terrace **241**

Firth of Forth

Bridge
Street

242

Portobello Promenade

247

Bath St

243

246

249

East Coast Railway

245

248

250

Brighton
Place

244

High Street

Abercorn Terrace

251

200m

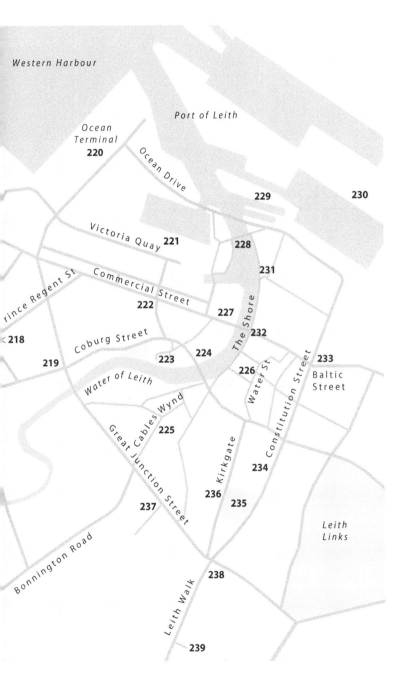

Western Harbour

Port of Leith

Ocean
Terminal
220

Ocean Drive

229

230

Victoria Quay **221**

228

231

Prince Regent St

Commercial Street

222

227

The Shore

232

Coburg Street

218

219

223

224

226

Water St

Constitution Street

233

Baltic
Street

Water of Leith

Great Cables Wynd

225

Kirkgate

234

Great Junction Street

236

235

237

Bonnington Road

Leith
Links

238

Leith Walk

239

212

Newhaven Harbour

Newhaven was settled in the 15th century by fisher folk crowded out of Leith, the seaport of Edinburgh. James IV established a royal dockyard in 1504. His flagship *The Great Michael,* the largest ship in Europe at the time, was launched here in 1511.

The harbour was enlarged in the 19th century. A ferry slip was built in 1812 and a drum-shaped harbour light (1830), followed by a breakwater (Robert Stevenson engineer 1864) and a cast iron lighthouse (1869). Fishing was the mainstay of the economy. The community was documented in the 1840s by pioneering photographers Hill and Adamson (see 78). Grainy images (the albums are in the National Portrait Gallery) show fishwives with baskets of herring, for sale on the streets of Edinburgh, and their menfolk mending nets by beached fish boats where the coast road is now.

Newhaven Harbour was never a serious rival to the Port of Leith, or Granton Harbour which opened in 1838. The fishery lasted until the 1950s, its heyday recalled by the Old Fish Market (1896), the timber building on the east quay; refurbished 2007 (Simpson & Brown Architects). Nearby, on the north-west edge of Leith's Western Harbour, is a shipwreck of speculative apartment blocks. They were part of a developer-led masterplan to 'regenerate' the post-industrial waterfront, rolled out before the 2008 financial crash.

213
Harbour Inn
4–6 Fishmarket Square

Most of old Newhaven was demolished in the 1960s. Two hundred families were evicted. Some were accommodated locally, in council housing which replaced 18th-century cottages branded slums.

Main Street never recovered from the loss of population and local shops. Some wynds and closes remain. The crowstep-gabled Harbour Inn is one of the few 18th-century buildings still here. Its gable-end faces the sea, a typical east coast feature, to protect homes from fierce weather. The best of the 1960s housing (Ian Lindsay & Partners) revived the vernacular style, with forestairs and harling on the exterior walls, pantiled roofs and gables. In 1977, Newhaven's surviving historic fabric was designated a conservation area, one of 50 at present in Edinburgh.

214
Starbank House
Starbank Park, 17 Laverockbank Road
1815

On the seaward slope below the house, where there is a panoramic view of the Firth of Forth, white stones were once laid to form a star said to symbolise the stars mariners navigated by. 'Starbank' is a wide-eaved villa with a doorway in picturesque 'Gothick' style, an eccentric relation to Gothic Revival. The pyramid-roofed bothy is Victorian. In 1889, Leith town council bought the property and opened the grounds as a public park. It is beautifully maintained by the Friends of Starbank Park supported by Edinburgh Parks Department.

215
Newhaven Station
85 Craighall Road

Almost all the railway lines in the suburbs of Edinburgh were closed in the 1960s by the Beeching cuts, which wiped out most branch lines in Britain. Many abandoned lines in the city have been repurposed as greenways

for cyclists and walkers. Newhaven Station (1879) served the Caledonian Railway line from Princes Street Station (see 121) to Leith. The timber building is supported on cast iron columns beside the road bridge; stairs led to the platforms below. It was restored (2010–14) to its original appearance by retired firefighter Richard Arnot, with office and co-working space inside.

216

Edinburgh Sculpture Workshop
21 Hawthornvale
> *Sutherland Hussey Harris Architects,*
> *David Narro Associates engineers, Rankin*
> *Fraser landscape design 2012; 2014*

Outstanding ensemble of creative, learning and event spaces constructed in two phases: the Bill Scott Sculpture Centre followed by the Creative Laboratories. The first is a robust concrete-floored, steel-framed structure with workshops and artists' studios. The second is softer, for research, exhibits and community engagement, with a café facing a courtyard. The centre was built on a disused railway yard where a free-standing *campanile*, illuminated at night, is a beacon for it.

217

Leith Fort
North Fort Street
> *James Craig 1780*

Built to defend Leith after John Paul Jones, the Scottish-born founder of the US Navy, led three warships into the Firth of Forth in 1779 during the American War of Independence. He intended to capture and hold Leith to ransom, but a storm sabotaged the plan and he sailed away.

The fort was an army base until 1956. It was redeveloped with council housing in the 1960s. The council blocks were demolished in 2012 and replaced with affordable, energy-efficient homes for Port of Leith Housing Association, to a design by Malcolm Fraser Architects inspired by the Victorian 'colonies' concept (see 143). The project was completed by Collective Architecture in 2018. The public realm (HarrisonStevens landscape design) incorporated cannons, a memory of the fort. Its guardhouses, gateway and stone walls are preserved on North Fort Street.

218
North Leith Parish Church
51 Madeira Street
William Burn 1816

Greek Revival church with a pedimented Ionic portico positioned to command the view from Prince Regent Street. Built to replace St Ninian's Church (see 223), which was too small for the growing congregation of North Leith Parish. Exceptional tiered clock tower – a crescendo of classical columns rising to a fluted needle spire and holy cross. The church was damaged during an air raid on Leith Docks in 1941 and renovated after the war.

219
Leith History Mural
North Junction Street at Ferry Road

A narrative of Leith before it was gentrified, painted on a tenement gable-end (Tim Chalk and Paul Grime artists 1986). The mural is next door to Leith Library and Theatre (1929–32), a civic centre built following the burgh's amalgamation in 1920 with Edinburgh, for which the centre's construction was a condition. The complex was known as Leith Town Hall but never used as such. A semicircular neoclassical colonnade behind the library leads to the long-derelict theatre, revived by Leith Theatre Trust for Edinburgh Festival events in 2018.

220

Ocean Terminal

Ocean Drive

Keppie Design architects, Conran Associates c. 2000

Ocean liner-size shopping mall on the site of Henry Robb shipyard which closed in 1984. It was the last of Leith's yards, ending a shipbuilding tradition that went back to medieval times. Ocean Terminal has a ship – the Royal Yacht *Britannia*, launched in 1953 at Clydebank, Glasgow. Forth Ports secured the right to display the relic of imperial travel and global prestige after it was decommissioned in 1997. It is one of Edinburgh's most popular attractions.

221

Victoria Quay

RMJM architects 1993–6

This is the Scottish Government's largest office block, built for the Scottish Office (see 76) on docklands developed in the early 19th century to enlarge the Port of Leith (John Rennie engineer). It is 250 metres long, with a superstructure like the deck and funnel of a great ship. Victoria Dock (c. 1850) is to the north. On the south side is Commercial Quay, lined with 19th-century bonded warehouses built to store whisky for export. The warehouses have been retrofitted with offices, co-working spaces, cafés and restaurants typical of Leith's post-industrial regeneration.

222

Mariners' Church

Dock Street

John Henderson c. 1840

Tudor-Gothic church, its seafaring connection symbolised by a carved longboat above the door. Leith Nautical College was launched here in 1855;

the building also served as the Seamen's Institute. The subsequent Nautical College (1903), now offices, is at 108 Commercial Street. In the lee of the church is the ruinous Citadel Archway (1656), the only remnant of Leith Citadel built by Cromwell after he invaded Scotland in 1650 to punish the Scots for proclaiming Charles II King in 1649.

223
St Ninian's Church and Manse
Quayside Street

The Abbott of Holyrood established a chapel here in 1493, rebuilt after the Reformation. In 1606, it became North Leith Parish Church with a manse attached. The Dutch-style belfry, a common type on Scotland's east coast, was built in 1675 (the date above the door). The manse was re-roofed and remodelled by William Adam (c.1735). The adjacent 18th-century tenement has a pend which led to the church. On the wall is an inscription, 'Blessed are they that hear the word of God and keep it.' In 1816, the congregation moved out (see 218). The property later became part of McGregor & Company's Quayside Mills.

The remains of St Ninian's were rehabilitated as offices (Simpson & Brown Architects 1998). The external 17th-century appearance was recreated (the correct limewash colour was revealed and reproduced) and the tower and clock restored. The gilded copper weathercock is a copy of the original in the National Museum of Scotland.

On Coburg Street is St Ninian's Churchyard (North Leith Churchyard). 'Burials from 1664–1820', says a sign at the gate, many of them mariners and merchants. Weathered gravestones, some with inscriptions eroded, others legible, are decorated with cherubs, skulls and crossbones, scrolls and ships' anchors. An obelisk (1815) is inscribed, 'Sacred to the Memory of William Gillespie, Harbour Master Leith.' Also here is the tomb of corn merchant Thomas Gladstone, grandfather of the political leader (see 126).

224
Ronaldson's Wharf
Sandport Place
DRD Architects, FBM Architects 2003;
2005
Award-winning development of
private and social housing. The two
private blocks came first, engaging with the Water of Leith Walkway and
Sandport Place; the social component, for Port of Leith Housing Association,
forms a convex curve into Sandport Way. Both types of tenure have wide
eaves and timber and stucco surfaces. The waterfront block has balconies
oriented for views and recessed for privacy; the top floor is a ripple of glass.
Stylish, outwardly egalitarian and clearly contemporary.

225
Cables Wynd House
Cables Wynd
Alison & Hutchison & Partners architects,
Blyth & Blyth engineers 1965
Brutalist slab block with a bendy bit, hence
the nickname 'the banana flats'. It was built
in tandem with Linksview House (north
foot of Kirkgate). Both were influenced by
Le Corbusier's Unite d'Habitation in Mar-
seilles. They were part of a post-war social
housing programme that transformed
much of urban Scotland. Cables Wynd featured in Irvine Welsh's novel *Trainspotting* (see also 238). In 2017, it was Grade A-listed by Historic Environment
Scotland for its architectural, social and cultural significance.

226
Lamb's House
11 Waters Close
1610; Groves-Raines Architects 2010–15
Named after 16th-century merchant Andro Lamb, who received Mary Queen
of Scots at his house when she returned to Scotland from France in 1561. It is

not known if this was the spot. The present house was built by members of Lamb's family. It is one the finest of its type and period in Scotland.

Crowstep gables, lime-rendered walls, timber balcony and a steeply pitched pantiled roof are characteristic features. Heavy timbers inside are original, imported from Norway or Sweden. Pantiles came from trade with the Hanseatic League (those on the recently renewed roof are antique, sourced in Sweden). The Renaissance-style garden, an office extension and ogee-roofed pavilion (respectively 17th- and 18th-century style) are pleasing interventions.

The house was rented to the burgesses of Edinburgh, who had exclusive mercantile rights to Leith Harbour. The ground floor was for trading; merchant tenants occupied the 6 flats accessed by a common stair – essentially, a tenement. In the 1930s, the 4th Marquess of Bute saved the house from demolition; in 1958, his son gave it to the National Trust for Scotland. In 2010, it was bought by conservation architects Kristin Hannesdottir and Nicholas Groves-Raines, who restored and rehabilitated it as a live/work dwelling. It won the Scottish Design Award for Re-Use of a Listed Building 2016.

227
Leith Customs House
65–67 Commercial Street
Robert Reid 1812; additions by
William Burn 1824
Leith was once Scotland's premier port, status that merited this Greek Revival, Doric-columned customs house, the oldest building of its type in the nation. Ship captains used to climb the balustraded forestair to declare their cargoes and pay duties. The previous customs house was at King's Wark (see 232). Royal authority is symbolised with lion and unicorn heraldry in the pediment. The interior (largely by William Burn) has a grand staircase leading to a gallery under a skylit dome. The landmark building was bought by the city in 2015. In 2019, the Scottish Historic Buildings Trust commissioned Richard Murphy Architects to visualise its future use for the community.

228
Victoria Swing Bridge
Alexander Rendel & George Robertson engineers 1871–4

Wrought iron, bowstring trussed bridge crossing the Water of Leith at Leith Docks. The hydraulically powered, counterweighted cantilevered span was the longest of its type in Britain. It was designed to swing open so ships could pass in and out of the Old Harbour. It carried two railway tracks which served Victoria Dock and Commercial Quay (see 221). It is now a pedestrian route and bikeway.

229
Prince of Wales Dock Pump House
Alexander Rendel engineer c.1860
Industrial infrastructure disguised as a Tuscan villa, a typical Victorian pretence. The building housed hydraulic pumps which powered the lock gates of the now disused and flooded Prince of Wales Dry Dock.

230
Port of Leith Grain Elevator
Imperial Dock
Some of Leith's street names – Baltic, Cadiz, Elbe, Madeira, for example – recall old trade links. Those links were broken when Scotland was drawn into English wars after the Union of the Crowns in 1603. Eventually, Leith's trade revived with access to the British Empire. Grain was a major import, for which Leith Dock Commission in 1934 built this concrete elevator (seen here from Albert Dock). It is heritage-listed for its local significance and modernist 'form follows function' aesthetic. It was decommissioned in 2006. Giant silos have been repurposed sustainably and creatively elsewhere. This one could be retrofitted as a vertical farm, but in 2015 Forth Ports sought and received planning permission to demolish it.

231
Merchant Navy
Memorial
Tower Place
Jill Watson artist,
Benjamin Tindall
Architects 2010

On the plaza outside the Malmaison Hotel is this sandstone column in the classical tradition commissioned by the Merchant Navy Memorial Trust. It commemorates the loss of more than 6,500 mariners from Scotland in war and at sea. Bronze reliefs and an interpretive panel recall the dangers seafarers faced and ships on which they served.

The Malmaison opened in 1994 as Leith's first boutique hotel. The Scots Baronial-style building was originally Leith Sailors' Home (Charles S S Johnston architect 1885). No other architectural site represents better the burgh's transition from tradition to trendiness. Nearby is the drum-shaped Signal Tower, built as a windmill (Robert Mylne 1685). From battlements added during the Napoleonic Wars, flags were flown to communicate tidal conditions to ships waiting to enter the harbour.

Sailing ships, fish nets and whalebones inspired the form of the Four

Winds Pedestrian Gates (1994) on the north side of Tower Place, where workers once entered the docks. The gates, designed and made at Ratho Byres Forge for Forth Ports, pivot on mast-like metal columns. The stone pillars and lamp with sea serpents were salvaged from the old gates.

On the quayside is the Whalers' Memorial – a harpoon gun from a ship owned by Leith-based Christian Salvesen whose Antarctic whaling fleet, before the First World War, was the largest in the world. Leith mariners hunted whales in the Arctic from the early 1600s until the mid 19th century, when the resource was depleted and whaling shifted to the south Atlantic.

232

Leith Old Harbour

The Shore

Coastal and sea-going sailing ships crowded the harbour until the mid 19th century, when deep-water docks were constructed for steamships. Crowstep-gabled old buildings (and some new ones in heritage style) line the east quayside, known as the Shore. The architecture is Scottish but the scene could be Hanseatic, reflecting old Leith's trade with continental Europe (photo, pages 154–155).

At number 28 the Shore is the former Old Ship Hotel (The Ship Inn of 1884). A carving of a ship, dated 1676, can be seen on one of its crowstep gables. Another ship (a 1984 replica; bracket a century older) sails out from the façade towards King's Landing. A plaque notes this is where in 1822 George IV disembarked (see 113). Number 35 the Shore (James Anderson Hamilton 1864) is Scots Baronial, decorated with bartizans, cannon spouts and a spire for its two griffins on Bernard Street to fly around.

At number 36 is King's Wark, an early 18th-century tenement and tavern with a prominent central gable. It was named after a commercial compound established by James I in 1434. King's Wark (in old Scots, meaning 'work') originally had a customs house, warehouses, accommodation for merchants, workshops for shipwrights and an armoury. The building was restored in the 1970s (Robert Hurd & Partners).

233

Leith Corn Exchange

Constitution and Baltic Streets

Peddie & Kinnear 1862

The Corn Exchange, capped with a cupola on a puffed-up dome, swaggers with 19th-century confidence. It contained chambers for merchants and a market hall with a clear-span timber and glass roof (in situ). On the Constitu-

tion Street façade, the grain trade is symbolised with *putti* engaged in agricultural and shipping activities on a Renaissance-style frieze (John Rhind sculptor). Nearby is the Robert Burns Memorial (David Watson Stevenson sculptor 1898), a bronze statue of the bard commissioned by Leith Burns Club (it was removed temporarily at the end of 2019 to make way for construction of the Edinburgh Trams extension to Newhaven).

Other buildings here from Leith's commercial heyday include the bow-fronted and domed Leith Bank, opened in 1806 at 25 Bernard Street (converted as a Buddhist meditation centre); the Italianate Royal Bank of Scotland (2 Bernard Street, 1872) and Leith Exchange (37–43 Constitution Street). The Exchange (Thomas Brown 1810) served the same purpose as the

Royal Exchange in Edinburgh (see 70), namely a meeting place for merchants. It included a coffee house, tavern and offices behind a dignified classical façade in the manner of Robert Adam. The wing on Assembly Street incorporated the old Assembly Rooms (1785).

234
Port of Leith Housing Association
108 Constitution Street
Lee Boyd Architects 2002

Contemporary design scaled to fit the historic urban context. White render nods to traditional harling. Timber alternates with glazing on the top deck, which is set back to visually reduce the building's height and bulk. Nautical feel, with *brise-soleil* rising to a sail-like canopy. The north corner is stone-clad, a courtesy to St Mary Star of the Sea next door. The Gothic Revival church (Edward Welby Pugin & Joseph Aloysius Hansom 1854) was named for Leith's patron saint. It has a collection of stained glass windows notable for numerous saints illustrated.

235

South Leith Parish Church

Kirkgate

15th century; Thomas Hamilton 1848

The 'Kirk of Leith' was larger than it is now because in 1560, during the Siege of Leith, the eastern section (the choir) was destroyed by English artillery.

The church of today dates from a radical rebuild in 1848. The west tower erected in the 17th century (similar to St Ninian's; see 223), demolished as unstable in 1836, was replaced in Gothic Revival style. The east and west gables were rebuilt, and later filled with Victorian stained glass from the Ballantine studio. The nave was reconstructed, gaining a spectacular oak hammerbeam roof. The Gothic tower and porch display the coats of arms of four successive Scottish monarchs: Queen Regent Mary of Guise (widow of James V), her daughter Mary Queen of Scots, James VI and Charles I. The burial ground too is a history lesson, with gravestones dating from the 17th century.

236

Trinity House

99 Kirkgate

Thomas Brown 1818

The maritime heritage of Leith is nowhere better seen and sensed than at Trinity House, a perfectly preserved Palladian villa. A hospital and almshouse were founded here in 1555 and a school of navigation in 1680, run by the Incorporation of Masters and Mariners of Leith. The charity maintained lighthouses, collected port dues and helped sailors and their families in need. Its coat of arms – two globes, anchor, compass and motto in Latin, meaning 'Men of virtue can master the stars, the land, the sea' – can be seen in the building's pediment.

The interior is atmospheric with ship models in glass cases, books, paintings, maps and charts and other memorabilia. There is a striking stained-glass war memorial window (1933) on the stair landing. The ceiling and frieze in the Conveying Room upstairs are decorated with Adamesque plasterwork showing Neptune, ancient mariners, sailing ships, navigational tools, flying fish and dolphins. Dominating the room is a canvas of 1842, *Vasco da Gama Encountering the Spirit of the Storm* by Edinburgh artist David Scott. Trinity House is managed by Historic Environment Scotland.

237
Dr Bell's School
101 Great Junction Street
Richard & Robert Dickson 1838

A statue of educational innovator Andrew Bell, who endowed the school, is set in a niche on the Tudor-Gothic façade (Peter Slater sculptor); also, a Leith School Board roundel with the ship and motto 'Persevere' from the burgh's coat of arms. In 1892, the board acquired the school from Bell's Trust and renamed it Great Junction Street School. A three-storey annex and a swimming pool were built (George Craig 1892; pool 1896). The latter is now an events venue. Behind the school, on Junction Place, is Victoria Baths (George Simpson), opened in 1899 and still in use. A finely carved example of Leith's coat of arms is in the pediment above the entrance.

238
Central Bar
Foot of Leith Walk
Peter Henderson c. 1900

Vintage interior featuring an ornate gantry with carved griffins, a Jacobean-style plaster ceiling and walls with mirrors and glazed ceramic tiles, some painted with sporting scenes – golf (played on Leith Links since the 16th century), yachting, hare coursing and grouse shooting. The bar was originally part of Leith Central Station (1898–1903), built by the North British Railway Company. The clock tower and Italianate façade were retained after the station was abandoned in the 1970s. Its derelict iron and glass train shed, since demolished, inspired a scene in and the title of the novel *Trainspotting*.

239
Raimes Clark & Co. (Lindsay & Gilmour Pharmacies)
19 Smith's Place

Palladian villa, the focal point of Smith's Place, a cul-de-sac laid out in 1814 by merchant James Smith. He built the villa and two terraces, anticipating the New Town would extend down Leith Walk. It didn't. In 1834, the property was sold by Smith's creditors to brothers John and Richard Raimes of Raimes Clark & Co., manufacturing and wholesale chemists. The house was occupied by the new owners. Laboratories, stables and a warehouse (now flats) were added in the courtyard.

The house remains the company office and archive (John Raimes started trading in the Old Town in 1816). Period features include a fanlight in New Town style, Venetian windows and a cantilevered oval staircase. Displayed in the vestibule is a metal model of a greyhound (another is on the weathervane), recalling the Raimes' prize-winning racing dogs.

240
Craigentinny Marbles (The Miller Mausoleum)
Craigentinny Crescent

David Rhind c. 1860; Alfred Gatley sculptor 1867
Roman grandeur next to a lawn bowling club in a 1920s suburb of bungalows. The 'marbles' are two panels of biblical scenes, 'The Overthrow of Pharaoh in the Red Sea' and 'The Song of Moses and Miriam'. The deceased was William Henry Miller of Craigentinny estate, a Member of Parliament in England, antiquarian and eccentric. He was buried in 1848, in a stone-lined vault he specified 12 metres below where the monument in memory of him was later erected.

241
Schultz Chocolate Factory
102 Inchview Terrace

J & J Hall architects; Edmund P Wells engineer 1906
Former Messrs. Schultz Continental Chocolate Factory, founded by German-

born merchant Charles William Schultz and run by his three Scottish-German sons. The reinforced concrete structure, advanced for its time, is concealed by a brick coating in Edwardian classical style.

German workers, mainly women, were employed until the First World War when the building was requisitioned under the Defence of the Realm Act for a barracks, and Schultz branded an 'enemy alien'. Two of his sons were killed serving with the British army in France. In 1922, the former factory became the WM Ramsay Technical Institute, rehabilitated as flats in 1995.

242

The Kilns

Bridge Street, Portobello

Portobello has an exceptionally rich and varied architectural heritage, often surprising, like these bottle kilns (1906; 1909), the only ones to survive in Scotland. They were part of the AW Buchan & Co. Thistle Pottery, which closed in 1972 after 200 years in business. It was one of several potteries established in Portobello where clay beds were discovered in the 18th century. Portobello Heritage Trust campaigned to save the kilns. The 1909 kiln was rebuilt in 2013 (the year is marked on a new brick). The 1906 kiln was subsequently dismantled for reconstruction in 2020.

243

Portobello Police Station

118 High Street

Robert Paterson 1877

This was Portobello's second Town Hall, also a public library and police station after the burgh merged with Edinburgh in 1896. The library relocated in 1963 and the police occupied the whole building. Scots Baronial style with crowstep gables, bartizans and a French tower with a cast iron crown and wrought iron weathervane.

The first town hall, Flemish style with griffin gargoyles (David Bryce 1863), stands at 189–193 High Street. It was built on the site of a shepherd's cottage of 1753, said to have been called 'Puerto Bello' by a tenant who had been at the capture of Puerto Bello, Panama by the Royal Navy in 1739, hence the burgh's name. The third (and current) town hall, 147–149 High Street, is an Edwardian classical-style building (James A Williamson 1914).

244
St John the Evangelist Catholic Church
35 Brighton Place

James Thomas Walford 1906

Soaring out of the douce 19th-century neighbourhood that is Brighton Park are the fantastic neo-Gothic pinnacles of St John's Church, like nothing the architect had done before and like nothing else in Edinburgh.

The nave, a conventional plan with arcaded aisles, is a powerful space – octagonal pillars with carved angels holding scrolls support the arches; light is beamed in from Gothic clerestories; the timber roof is a boat-shaped barrel vault. The chancel glows with stained glass windows (Edward Frampton artist) illustrating the Nativity, Crucifixion and Resurrection. The altar, with a painting of The Last Supper, was designed by the architect who, being a member of the church and nearing the end of his career, waived his fee.

245
Rosefield Avenue Lane

Haar Architects 2014

An old stable in a former coal merchant's yard, converted in the 1980s, refurbished and extended as a contemporary laneway house. Utilitarian aesthetic with larch cladding and some original brickwork. The elevation greets the lane warmly but grants privacy to the living spaces and a walled garden. Saltire Society Award winner 2015, one of several innovative laneway dwellings in Portobello (see 248).

246

The George Cinema

14 Bath Street

Thomas Bowhill Gibson 1939

Streamline Moderne, originally with a spectacular glazed central tower, like a beacon

taller than the neighbouring tenement. Opened as the County Cinema with
a screening of Disney's *Snow White and the Seven Dwarfs*. Renamed The
George in 1954; later a bingo hall. Planning permission for façade retention
and demolition of the rest of the heritage-listed building for residential redevelopment was refused in 2018. Architect Gibson designed the Dominion,
Morningside (see 177).

247

26BS (26 Bath Street)

John Kinsley Architects 2017

A progressive self-build project
planned and procured by the
families that live here. It re-imagines
the Scottish tenement typology, an
example of which is next door. The

façade fits the height of the tenement and steps down with courtesy to the
other neighbour, a 19th-century terrace. Cladding is mainly sandstone; zinc
at the rear where there is a communal garden.

The structure is eco-friendly cross-laminated timber, manufactured
off-site. It was erected in nine days by three joiners. Renewable energy is
sourced and insulation is to Passivhaus standards. The project has won
awards, among them the Wood for Good/Forestry Commission Scotland
Award for the Best Use of Timber (RIAS Awards 2018).

248

Japanese House

11a Bellfield Lane

Konishi Gaffney Architects 2009

Portobello's lanes are a collage of cottages, garages, old workshops and stables. Thoughtfully designed new buildings fit the diversity, like this timber-

framed, energy-efficient self-build, by and for the architects. Seen from the lane, the house is contemporary Scottish vernacular with oak cladding. Concealed from the passerby is a seamless, very Japanese transition from minimalist open-plan living space to the walled garden.

At the foot of the lane is the Ramp House (Chambers McMillan Architects 2012), steel-framed behind a façade of stone and shingles, so-called because it is entirely wheelchair-friendly.

249
Portobello Swim Centre
Portobello Promenade (at Bellfield Street)
Robert Morham, City Architect 1898–1901

Recently restored Victorian public baths facing the sea on Portobello Promenade. Opened as Portobello Sea Water Baths, they were 'the most modern in Britain', with men's and women's heated pools and Turkish baths. All in situ, well preserved and popular. Scottish Renaissance-style façade with Dutch gables, sea-view balconies and carved coats of arms of Portobello and Edinburgh.

250
Portobello Old Parish Church
16b Bellfield Street
William Sibbald 1809

Georgian elevation with a delicate fanlight in the doorway, elegantly carved date stone, and Gothic tracery in the upper windows. Clock tower (1839) with Roman Doric pilasters, octagonal belfry, cupola and weathercock. Spacious sanctuary with a north gallery (1878) on cast iron Corinthian columns. Beside

the church is a compact Victorian graveyard and a modernist hall (Alan Reiach & Partners 1964).

When the congregation relocated in 2014 to Portobello & Joppa Parish Church, the property was threatened with residential redevelopment. This was prevented, thanks to grass roots action which invoked the Scottish Government's community right-to-buy legislation, the first time it was used in an urban location. The church and hall were renamed 'Bellfield' and reopened as a community centre in 2018.

251
Portobello & Joppa Parish Church
1 Brunstane Road North
John Honeyman 1877; James G Cuthbertson 2001

Originally St Philip's Parish Church, designed in Gothic Revival style by Glasgow architect Honeyman. In 1906, the firm Honeyman, Keppie & Mackintosh built a chancel for a new organ, for which Charles Rennie Mackintosh designed a Gothic timber screen, unfortunately removed in the 1960s. It is unlikely it would have survived the fire which destroyed the timber roof and scorched the interior in 1998. Firefighters contained the blaze. The stone structure, tower and steeple were saved.

Reconstruction kept the original stone arcades and aisles in the nave but reconfigured the space for contemporary worship. The outstanding feature is two stained and painted glass windows (Douglas Hogg artist) which replaced those fatally damaged by the fire. They won the Saltire Society Art and Crafts in Architecture Award 2003.

The three bridges

The Forth estuary is unique, having three bridges side by side spanning three centuries: the Forth Railway Bridge (1890), the Forth Road Bridge (1964) and Queensferry Crossing (2017). Each represents the engineering expertise of its era, respectively cantilever, suspension and cable-stayed.

The bridges link the villages of South and North Queensferry. The names recall Queen Margaret and the ferry service she endowed in the 11th century for free passage of pilgrims to the Kingdom of Fife. The ferry shortened the journey to St Andrews and Dunfermline, places of pilgrimage in medieval times, and between the royal palace at Dunfermline and Edinburgh Castle.

6

Out of Town

Duddingston Kirk—Robin Chapel—Craigmillar Castle—Bridgend Farm—Rosslyn Chapel—Craiglockhart Hospital—Saughton Park— Water of Leith Visitor Centre—Colinton Parish Church—Oriam Sports Performance Centre—Jupiter Artland—Edinburgh Airport Control Tower—Corstorphine Old Parish Church—St Anne's Parish Church— Lauriston Castle—Cramond—Dalmeny Kirk—The Forth Bridges— Hopetoun House

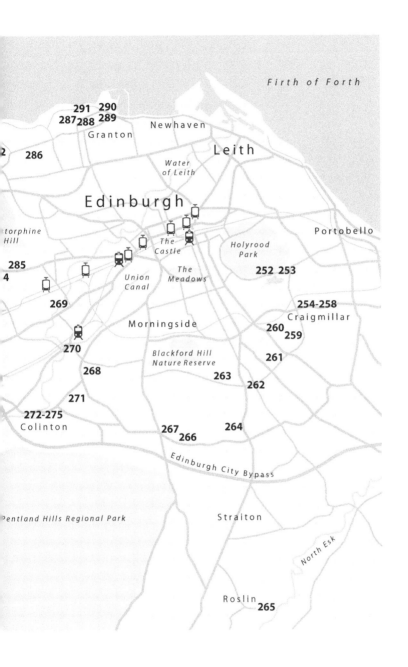

252
Duddingston Kirk
Old Church Lane
Duddingston Village
12th century
One of the oldest parish churches in Scotland still used for worship. It dates from the mid 12th century when David I granted the land to the Abbott of Kelso Abbey, extending the abbey's estate in the Borders to the edge of Edinburgh.

The oldest feature is the original entrance, a Romanesque round-arched doorway on the south wall. Inside, a chevron-patterned arch divides the nave from the chancel. In 1631, the north wall was replaced with new entrance and a gallery funded by a local laird, whose duty it was (along with poor relief and other social commitments common at the time). The belfry dates from 1825. The kirk was restored by Robert Rowand Anderson in 1889. The 19th-century gatehouse, styled like a castle keep, was built as a lookout to foil body-snatchers from Edinburgh.

In Duddingston Village is the Bonnie Prince Charlie House (number 8 The Causeway; early 18th century) where in 1745 the prince held his council of war the night before beating British government troops at the Battle of Prestonpans. At 43–45 The Causeway is the 14th-century Sheep Heid Inn, reputed to be the oldest in Scotland. The village, below Arthur's Seat, hugs the shore of Duddingston Loch, a wildlife reserve since 1923. The setting could be the Highlands, not 3 kilometres from Princes Street.

253
Thomson's Tower
Dr Neil's Garden, Old Church Lane
William Playfair 1825
Designed for the Duddingston Curling Society, with storage for its curling stones on the ground floor. Above was a studio for the Reverend John Thomson, landscape painter and minister at Duddingston Kirk. He was a friend of Henry

Raeburn who painted a memorable image of Duddingston Loch, *The Skating Minister* (c. 1795), now in the Scottish National Gallery. The garden, on land previously used for grazing, was begun in 1963 by two doctors, Nancy and Andrew Neil. Since 1997, it has been cared for by Dr Neil's Garden Trust, which restored the tower in 2009 (Simpson & Brown Architects). The wooded garden steps down enigmatically to the loch. A treasure.

254
Drybrough's Craigmillar Brewery
146 Duddingston Road West
Robert Hamilton Paterson 1892
Edinburgh was once the brewing capital of Scotland. Canongate, Fountainbridge and Craigmillar were centres of the industry. Drybrough's, founded in the 18th century, was the oldest brewery. It closed in 1987. Its historic site is now home to several independent businesses, notably Holyrood Architectural Salvage. At Peffer Bank nearby is the head brewer's house; tenements on Peffer Place housed brewery workers.

255
Castlebrae Business Centre
40 Peffer Place
Reid & Forbes 1935
Two similar parallel blocks, the north one with an Art Deco tower, originally Niddrie Marischal School. Classrooms were generously glazed and cross-ventilated to be bright and salubrious. Reinforced concrete construction, horizontal windows, white stucco walls and the tower are typical of the Moderne style, usually applied to cinemas and office buildings on industrial estates. Refurbished in 2016 as a community business centre.

256
Craigmillar Library (East Neighbourhood Centre)
101 Niddrie Mains Road
City of Edinburgh Council (architects), Graham Construction 2012
Craigmillar was a 1930s council housing scheme of three-storey walk-ups

notorious for multiple deprivation after local mines and breweries which provided work closed. The run-down council blocks were demolished, replaced with mixed-tenure contemporary housing designed to create a sense of pride and place. Civic presence materialised with this one-stop community and library hub, a symbol of the fresh start. The colonnade of slender columns recalls classical tradition. Energy efficient, rated BREEAM Excellent.

On Moffat Way is the joint campus of Niddrie Mill & St Francis Primary Schools (Elder & Cannon Architects 2008). This new school and its traffic-calmed, landscaped neighbourhood evolved from a masterplan, the Craigmillar Urban Design Framework (2005), influenced by the doctrine of 'new urbanism' which guided the regeneration.

257

Thistle Foundation Centre of Wellbeing
Queen's Walk
3DReid Architects 2016
Community centre in a village of white-washed row houses (c. 1950) built by the Thistle Foundation to help disabled ex-service personnel live independently. The charity continues to support people living with long-term health issues. Spaces in the new building are daylit, uncluttered, flexible for exercise, therapy, meetings and conferences, centred around a bright and welcoming reception hub. Award-winning use of timber inside and out. The name neatly formed in the timber cladding reflects the depth of the cross in the stone-work at the Thistle Foundation's nearby Robin Chapel.

258
Robin Chapel
Thistle Foundation, Queen's Walk
John Fraser Matthew 1950–3
Memorial chapel commissioned by the parents of Lieutenant Robin Tudsbery

of the Royal Horse Guards who was killed in action a few days before the end of the Second World War. Its architect had been in partnership with Robert Lorimer, whose Scottish vernacular and Arts & Crafts sensibility was evidently influential. The chapel's west front is rusticated. There is a stained glass cross set in masonry patterned like a sunburst. The medieval-style belfry is partly crow-stepped. The sanctuary is roofed with ancient Ballachulish slate. The ceiling inside is plaster, barrel-vaulted. Woodwork is East Lothian oak, with pew-ends and the pulpit featuring carved

animals and birds. Every item is beautifully crafted.

Robin Tudsbery was a nature-lover, but in the glorious east window (Sadie McLellan artist) he is cavalry officer, stylised in stained glass as a Roman charioteer. Other windows (same artist 1952–4) were inspired by *The Pilgrim's Progress*. Outside, doves of peace and a robin are perched on the wrought iron finial.

259
Craigmillar Castle
Craigmillar Castle Road
14th–17th centuries

A ruin since the 18th century, 'Edinburgh's other castle' is layered with 16th- and 17th-century accretions extending from the core, a 14th-century tower house with some walls almost three metres thick. An outer courtyard was added in the 15th century, protected by massive machiolated walls and flanking towers. The fortress was built by the Prestons of Craigmillar whose property it was from 1374 to 1660. In 1544, during the wars of the 'rough wooing' (see 2), it was surrendered without a fight to the Earl of Hertford. Hertford's troops set it ablaze, sacked Edinburgh and tried to capture the castle there. Craigmillar was repaired but abandoned in the 18th century.

Family life was focused around the hearth in the vaulted Great Hall, a

double-height space surrounded by a claustrophobic vertical maze of ancillary rooms and spiral stairs. Footsteps and voices of unseen visitors are mysteriously amplified, or are they ghosts?

Association with Mary Queen of Scots adds frisson to Craigmillar's empty spaces. It was here in 1566 that the Earl of Bothwell and fellow conspirators are said to have planned the murder of Mary's second husband, Lord Darnley. After the deed was done – gunpowder bomb in a house in the Old Town – she married Bothwell. Her presence with a retinue of French courtiers gave the area around the castle the name 'Little France'. Craigmillar Castle and Edinburgh Castle are managed by Historic Environment Scotland.

260
Bridgend Farm
41 Old Dalkeith Road
c. 1750; extended c. 1830; rehabilitated, Malcolm Fraser Architects, Halliday Fraser Munro architects 2018

Lowland Scottish farmhouse, yard and vegetable garden on a farm like many others that once fed the city. The land was part of Craigmillar Castle estate. There was a chapel (1518), now a ruin (a similar chapel can be seen at the castle). The city could have sold the property for commercial development. Instead, a civic asset transfer to the community prevailed.

The site has been transformed by the architects and volunteers as an activity and learning centre, with an emphasis on sustainability. There is a café, kitchen and a meeting room. A lift makes the house mobility-friendly (original stone stair in situ). Outside, there are events and play areas, a stage and marquee. There is a row of new timber-framed, charred-larch-clad workshops designed by Malcolm Fraser; also a timber-framed, straw-bale, lime-rendered eco-bothy (Duncan Roberts architect 2020). A delight, as is everything here. The regeneration won a Scottish Design Award 2020.

261
Craigend Park
84 Kingston Avenue
Frederick Thomas Pilkington 1869
Pilkington was a wizard of creepy Victorian Gothic. By day, his buildings are simply strange, at night sinister. Craigend has all the trimmings: spiky tower, carved cornucopia, chimera on a drainpipe, Green Man above the loggia, and a wood-panelled hall with a baronial staircase and domed skylight. It was built for William Christie, a tailor with business premises on George Street. From 1918 to 1925 it was a hospital for shell-shocked soldiers; later Kingston Clinic for alternative medical therapy. In the 1980s it was subdivided for flats.

262
Liberton Kirk
Kirkgate
James Gillespie Graham 1815
Early Gothic Revival church with a landmark pinnacled tower, and crenellated parapets on ivy-covered walls and gables. The kirk's recorded history goes back to the reign of David I, when it was a dependent chapel of St Cuthbert's (see 120). It is thought to have been a Christian site long before then because, in the 19th century, two ancient Celtic crosses were found in the kirkyard. The medieval building was demolished in 1815. Gillespie Graham's replacement was funded by the 'heritors' (the feudal landowners of the parish).

263
Liberton Tower
Liberton Tower Lane
A tower house (c. 1450) abandoned around 1600 when the owner, William Little, a Lord Provost of Edinburgh, built Liberton House nearby. Liberton Tower is thought to have been bombarded by artillery during Cromwell's

campaign in 1650. Thereafter, is was used as a barn for farm animals and feed. In 1998, it was restored and rehabilitated for vacation rental (Simpson & Brown Architects). Floors and the external timber stair were reinstated (the original stair would have had a drawbridge at the top). Harling and limewash were applied, guided by on-site investigation of the surviving fabric. William Little's Liberton House, on the south side of Liberton Drive, was restored in 1997 (Groves-Raines Architects).

264
Mortonhall Crematorium
Howden Hall Road
Basil Spence, Glover & Ferguson 1967
The real world recedes on the path through woodland to a clearing where this secular starship waits to spirit the dead away. The Main Chapel is an austere, contemplative space with a central aisle along which coffin bearers carry their load. The space narrows to focus on a chancel-like, top-lit void expressed outside as a spire. Exterior walls are vertical slabs with narrow strips of stained glass between them, reminiscent of the architect's Coventry Cathedral. The windows cast coloured patterns on the chapel's white plaster walls. The palette of materials throughout is restrained – timber, flint aggregate masonry, concrete. Spence achieved timelessness here. The building will never grow old.

265
Rosslyn Chapel
Chapel Loan, Roslin Village
It took 40 years for skilled workers, many 'from other regions and foreign kingdoms', to construct and decorate Rosslyn Chapel, begun in 1446

by William St Clair as place of worship for his family. The exterior is awash with Gothic tracery, flying buttresses and pinnacles. Excavations in the 19th century revealed foundations thought to indicate a cruciform plan. These would have made the chapel twice the size, but William died in 1484 and with him the more ambitious design.

After the Reformation, the chapel was branded by Protestant zealots a 'house and monument of idolatrie', sacked and abandoned. In 1862, the 3rd Earl of Rosslyn restored it for Episcopalian worship (David Bryce architect). In 1995, the Rosslyn Chapel Trust was formed to conserve the building and protect its hinterland. Inside, there is a deluge of decoration. Almost every surface is covered with medieval stone carvings of exceptional quality, notably the ceiling above the nave, the Apprentice Pillar (said to be haunted by the ghost of the boy who carved it), and angels playing musical instruments, including bagpipes.

Rosslyn became an iconic attraction after being featured in the 2003 novel and subsequent film *The Da Vinci Code*, which popularised long-held speculation that the chapel is linked to the Knights Templar and the Holy Grail. 'The most mysterious and magical chapel on earth', the book's author Dan Brown said. Rosslyn received record numbers of sightseers – and funds for conservation and a Visitor Centre (Page\Park Architects, Elliott &

Company engineers, Ian White Associates landscape design 2011). The centre is an oak-framed pavilion, clearly contemporary but in harmony with the historic religious and rural setting. An adjacent stone building was incorporated, its shape echoed in the new structure.

Nearby is the St Clair's 15th-century Rosslyn Castle, a romantic ruin above Roslin Glen.

266
Princess Gate
Margaret Rose Avenue
Malcolm Fraser Architects 2006

Award-winning housing on the site of Princess Margaret Rose Hospital, closed in 2000. The hospital had a modernist extension (Morris & Steedman 1966). City planners wanted any new-build to achieve similar quality. The developer had to hire a good architect. The timber-framed two-level blocks, each with three or four units, step down the sloping site. Gardens face south, front doors and parking are on the north sides. For views of the Pentland Hills, living spaces are upstairs, like those at the Sillitto House (see 184). Palette unpretentious, simply white-harled masonry and timber cladding.

267
Fairmilehead Parish Church
1a Frogston Road West
Leslie Grahame Thomson 1938

Ogee-roofed gabled tower with a Nordic as much as Scottish Arts and Crafts character. Even more Scandinavian inside. The plan is conventional – cruciform with nave, vaulted transepts and apse – but the space is minimalist and column-free with a white-rendered parabolic ceiling. Stained glass windows (four by artist William Wilson) are virtually the only decoration. The effect is ethereal, extraordinarily modern for Edinburgh of the time and still a surprise.

268
Craiglockhart Hospital
Edinburgh Napier University
219 Colinton Road
Peddie & Kinnear 1877–80

During the First World War this was an army hospital where officers were treated for psycho-logical stress and shell shock. Among them were the soldier poets Wilfred

Owen, and Siegfried Sassoon who recalled it 'sepulchral and oppressive, re-deemed only by its healthy situation and pleasant view of the Pentland Hills.'

Originally it was a hydropathic hospital built in Italianate style. After the Second World War, until 1984, it was the Convent of the Sacred Heart and a teacher training college. It is now Napier University's Business School. Displayed inside is the university's War Poets Collection.

269

Saughton Park

Balgreen Road

Sutherland Hussey Harris Architects,
Richard Shorter Architect, David Narro
Associates engineers, Ironside Farrar
landscape design 2019

This was a 17th-century country estate bought by Edinburgh Corporation in 1900 to create a public park. In 1908, the Scottish National Exhibition of agriculture, engineering and horticulture was held here. Exhibition Bridge spans the Water of Leith at Gorgie Road, but the glory days faded and the park decayed.

It has been revived by the city in partnership with the Royal Caledonian Horticultural Society and Friends of Saughton Park. The cast iron Lion Foundry bandstand (1909), removed in the 1980s and stored in pieces, has been reassembled. The Royal Promenade (1908), the Walled Garden (1850s) and its heritage-listed stone sundial, and the glasshouse have been restored. There is a traditional physic garden. The Stable Block, with a modern addition, is now a community venue, café and base for the RCHS. Micro-hydro technology (SP Energy Networks) on the Water of Leith generates all the electricity the park requires, making Saughton 'the first fully eco-powered greenspace in the UK'.

270

Water of Leith Visitor Centre

24 Lanark Road

Malcolm Fraser Architects 2000

The Water of Leith, 'a silver thread in a ribbon of green' flows for 35 kilometres from its source in the Pentland Hills to the sea at Leith. It was once industrial along much of its length. Dozens of mills produced, variously, cloth, paper, lumber, flour and snuff, and polluted the water. The environment has since recovered. Its natural habitat and history are explained in the centre, run by the Water of Leith Conservation Trust, established in 1988. The venue is a renovated but externally unaltered Victorian school house to which was added a timber extension astride the Water of Leith Walkway.

Downstream are two bridges: Slateford Aqueduct (1822) and Slateford Viaduct (1848), constructed for the Union Canal and the Caledonian Railway.

271
Redford Barracks
Colinton Road
Harry Bell Measures 1909–15
The largest facility for the British army constructed in Scotland since Fort George near Inverness was built after the Jacobite Rising of 1745. Two mighty French Renaissance-style barrack blocks face Colinton Road. The east one was the Cavalry Barracks; the west, the Infantry Barracks. Edinburgh Castle's garrison moved here in 1923. Redford has traditionally provided rehearsal space and accommodation for performers during the Edinburgh Military Tattoo. The MoD (Ministry of Defence) intends to close the barracks and dispose of the property.

272
St Cuthbert's Episcopal Church
Westgarth Avenue at Colinton Road
Robert Rowand Anderson 1888–94
Delightful blend of Scots Gothic and Arts and Crafts styles. The architect was a founding member of the church and a generous sponsor. He designed almost everything here, from the 17th-century-style belfry decorated with floral brackets and gargoyles to the painted timber ceilings inspired by 16th-century examples in the Old Town. He lived nearby

at 'Allermuir' (15 Woodhall Road), a Scots Baronial villa he designed (1879). His townhouse was at Rutland Square (see 124).

273
Colinton Parish Church
Dell Road
Sydney Mitchell 1908

The church replaced an unlovely 1771 rebuild of the 17th-century kirk (the parish was founded in the 11th century). The *campanile* (David Bryce 1837) was taken down and reconstructed. Decorative Celtic angels glide above the columns in the nave. The apse is Byzantine, half-domed, with stained glass windows and a wall with Art Nouveau stencilled vine patterns.

Outside, there is a statue of Robert Louis Stevenson as a boy (Alan Herriot sculptor 2013), commissioned by Colinton Community Conservation Trust. RLS often visited his grandfather, Lewis Balfour, the minister at Colinton, and wrote poems, *A Child's Garden of Verses*, inspired in part from his time here. In the kirkyard's row of mausoleums (on the north side of the kirk) is the Balfour family tomb, and that of James Gillespie of Spylaw House.

274
Spylaw House
Spylaw Park, 25 Spylaw Street
c. 1650 (mill); 1773 (house)

Hidden in a glen of the Water of Leith is this charming Georgian house incorporating the remains of Spylaw Mill. The site, now a public park, belonged to James Gillespie who made a fortune as a snuff manufacturer and tobacco dealer (a plaque at 231 High Street on the Royal Mile marks where he and his brother had a shop). In 1797, he bequeathed to the Merchant Company his Colinton estate and money to build and endow a hospital for the elderly and, for poor boys, a free school, now James Gillespie's High School (see 168).

His philanthropy, like much of the period, is tainted by slavery. The tobacco he traded was imported from plantations in Virginia worked by

African slaves. He was not alone. In 18th-century Britain, people working in almost all occupations were sustained directly or indirectly by colonialism and the plantation economy.

275

Colinton Tunnel

Water of Leith Walkway

1874; Colinton Tunnel Project 2020

Scotland's longest heritage mural decorates the tunnel, which was part of the Caledonian Railway line from Princes Street Station to Balerno. Passenger trains ceased in 1943, and freight in 1967 when the line was abandoned. It has since become part of the Water of Leith Walkway.

Artist Chris Rutterford and a team of muralists, school children and other volunteers created the local history artwork. Robert Louis Stevenson's poem 'From a Railway Carriage' inspired the narrative. His verse is featured on the mural – so is he, at his writing desk and looking out from a railway carriage.

276

Oriam, Scotland's Sports Performance Centre

Heriot-Watt University

Reiach & Hall Architects, Engenuiti engineers, Rankin Fraser landscape design 2016

The national training centre for football; also used by the national rugby team and for other sports. A full-size soccer pitch is under the translucent PVC fabric roof, which is tempered to limit solar gain and tensioned across an arched steel frame said to have been inspired by the trajectory of a famous free kick. Parallel to this is an indoor sports hall. The corridor between the two is defined by a heritage-listed stone wall, part of a walled garden previously here.

'Oriam' means 'I am gold' in Gaelic. The ambition is to train players to the highest standards. As a work of architecture and engineering, the building achieves them.

277

Linburn Centre

Louis Braille Avenue, Wilkieston

Page\Park Architects, Ian White Associates landscape design 2011

Scottish War Blinded was established in Edinburgh in 1915 to aid veterans blinded during the First World War. The charity, needing more space during the Second World War, moved out to Linburn estate. Cottages and workshops were built in the peaceful landscape (Lorimer & Matthew c. 1944). Page\Park's eco-friendly new building was the first phase of a two-part development designed for the visually impaired to navigate without stress. Phase two (2015) added housing and a sports hall in a cluster of smaller buildings equally sensitive to users' needs and comfort.

278

Bonnington House

Wilkieston

An eighteenth-century country house remodelled tastefully in 1858 in Jacobean style. According to a map (c. 1763), the property had two wings. In 2015, the lost symmetry was revived by Benjamin Tindall Architects. The shift from old to new is subtle but clear, and craftsmanship exceptional. Jacobean style notwithstanding, the effect is classical, Palladian.

The new 'ballroom' wing and a 16th-century doocot are occasionally open to the visitors at Jupiter Artland (next entry). Exhibitions can be held in the ballroom, which has a decorated plasterwork ceiling by Naomi Jobson and Bob Moore (2015) inspired by the four seasons. The formal avenue leading to the house was reinstated. Benjamin Tindall Architects also produced the masterplan that guided Jupiter Artland's landscape design.

279
Jupiter Artland
Bonnington House Steadings, Wilkieston

Enchanting art park opened in 2009 by the owners of Bonnington House. Their vision was to get art out of the house, *en plein air* for everyone. This is done well at the National Galleries on Belford Road (see 135) but space there is limited. Here there is a landscape – acres of it – and artworks are everywhere.

There is an earthwork, *Cells of Life* by Charles Jencks, and *Love Bomb* (Marc Quinn), a 12-metre high orchid surreal like the 19th-century curiosities on Calton Hill. *Rose Walk* (Pablo Bronstein) is a lattice-fenced pathway with a gazebo at each end – one chinoiserie, the other Gothic – a play on the fashion since the Renaissance for eccentric and exotic garden follies. The classical theme in landscape design is recalled in the *Temple of Apollo* (Ian Hamilton Finlay). There are many more pieces, and new works appear as if by magic.

The derelict steading at Bonnington House was repurposed for temporary exhibitions and as a café/restaurant (Benjamin Tindall Architects 2009). In

the yard is an icon of American 20th-century design – a Silver Streak Clipper trailer, refitted as a food truck. The art park is completely informal. Jupiter is the Roman god of the sky. Under it here you can roam. The pleasure is simply in looking and of discovery.

280

Edinburgh Airport Control Tower

3DReid Architects, Arup engineers 2005

The airport was originally a First World War airfield, later RAF Turnhouse, home of 603 (City of Edinburgh) Squadron. A Second World War memorial (a replica Spitfire) is beside the approach road to the terminal. Commercial flights started in 1947.

The old terminal (1977) has been superseded by periodic new construction. Only one structure is worth seeing and it is a tour de force – the air traffic control tower. The sculptural form, clad in diamond-shaped aluminium panels, conceals a 7-metre diameter concrete service core. At the top is a floor slab on which the control room is perched. The tower is 57 metres high, to afford controllers a 360° view. At night LED luminaries colour the iconic structure, which inspired a new logo for the airport.

281

Royal Bank of Scotland Gogarburn
175 Glasgow Road

Michael Laird Architects, RHWL Architects, Anthony Hunt Associates engineers, EDAW landscape design 2002–5

A 19th-century country estate (later a hospital site) redeveloped as RBS World Headquarters, before the financial crash and the bank's meltdown in 2008. The centrepiece is a linear mega block with wings perpendicular to a spine conceived as a village street, a skylit focus for the several thousand staff here. The campus is set in the parkland of Gogarburn House (c. 1816, rebuilt 1893). A staff recreation centre was built behind the house, the stables became a nursery, and a conference centre was opened nearby. Proximity to Edinburgh Airport, links to public transport and the mature landscape made the site attractive. To ease access, a parabolic-arched bridge was constructed, spanning the Glasgow Road.

282
Edinburgh Park
South Gyle

*Richard Meier & Partners, masterplan 1991–3; Ian White Associates
landscape design*

Extensive north American-style business park developed by the city's EDI

Group. The intent was to develop a zone for investment outside the World Heritage Site and maintain Edinburgh's status as a global financial and national administrative centre.

The office buildings are functional,

energy-efficient, some by distinguished architects. Notable are Alexander Graham Bell House for British Telecom at 1 Lochside View (Bennetts Associates architects 1999), named to honour the inventor of the telephone, and the JP Morgan Building at 3 Lochside View (Gordon Murray + Alan Dunlop Architects 2001).

Landscape design was a significant part of the masterplan. There are tree-lined boulevards, even lochans, creating an eco-friendly environment for workers and wildlife (the first arrival was a swan). There is public art. The largest piece is *The Wealth of Nations* (Eduardo Paolozzi 1993), commissioned

by the Royal Bank of Scotland and installed outside Drummond House. Giant hands on the levers of power suggest not a banker but a creator. Inscribed is a quote from Albert Einstein: 'Knowledge is wonderful, but imagination is even better.'

283

Craigsbank Church

19 Craigs Bank

Rowand Anderson, Kininmonth & Paul
1966; refurbished LDN Architects 2009

The kirk was founded by the Church of Scotland in 1937. Post-war, the congregation outgrew its traditional-style stone building (now the church hall). More space was provided in this white-rendered modernist box, its concave bell tower like a sail on the community's sea of 1920s bungalows.

The minimalist aesthetic is moored to the past – the sunken sanctuary is said to symbolise the hidden hillside hollows where Covenanters worshipped during the 'killing times' of the 17th century. The serene, square-plan space has aisles for circulation above seating tiered on three sides; pulpit, crucifix and church organ are on the fourth side. Natural light is distributed indirectly from the fringes of a suspended 'floating' ceiling. Ingenious and inspired.

284

Corstorphine Old Parish Church

Kirk Loan

Rooted in an early 15th-century family chapel built by the laird of Corstorphine, merchant and burgess Adam Forrester, Lord Provost of Edinburgh. Its outward appearance today dates from additions made in 1429 by his son. Beside it stood a 12th-century kirk demolished in 1646; some stones from it are thought to have been recycled in the west porch, the entrance to the church.

The square tower houses a bell cast in 1728. The stone spire was a landmark in the farmland which surrounded Corstorphine village until the 20th century. The north transept (1646) was enlarged in 1828 by William Burn, who reclad St Giles' High Kirk. The vaulted nave was reconstructed (George Henderson 1905) in concrete rather than stone, and replica stone-slabbed roofs fitted (those on the east choir and sacristy are original). Superb stained glass South Window (Gordon Webster artist 1970); other stained glass by Ballantine (1905). Below Webster's window is a finely carved effigy: a knight in armour, one of the Forresters, with a dog by his feet. More effigies are in niches in the north wall of the chancel. Superficial damage was likely caused by Cromwell's troops billeted here in 1650.

Outside, above the east window, is a lamp in a niche. It is still lit, a tradition since medieval times when the light at night guided travellers, or villagers home. They would have passed the Forresters' 14th-century castle (demolished 1797), a loch (since drained), the beehive-shaped Corstorphine Doocot (2 Dovecot Road) and the Dower House, now Corstorphine Heritage Centre in St Margaret's Park (both buildings 16th century). Cottages by the doocot once housed Dovecot Studios (see 33).

285
St Anne's Parish Church
1 Kames Road at St John's Road
Peter Macgregor Chalmers 1913

A 'daughter church' of Corstorphine Old Parish Church, established in 1903 in a timber-framed and corrugated iron-roofed 'Tin Kirk'. The temporary structure was replaced by this beautifully crafted and almost complete Romanesque Revival building. The only omission is the *campanile* to have been erected above the entrance, not built due to the outbreak of the First World War.

St Anne's is a traditional stone-built church. The porch, with carved figures of Christ, the four evangelists, angels and the signs of the zodiac, leads to an arcaded nave with clerestory windows and apse, as if in Ravenna.

It was desired that 'the stones speak' – the capitals on the columns to the aisles are crisply carved expressions of biblical themes. The floor of the apse is marble (the lighter stone from Greece; the darker from Iona). Above are three stained glass windows by Alfred Webster, installed in 1917 (he never saw them in situ, having been killed on active service in France in 1915). The scheme was completed in 1953, with two flanking windows by his son Gordon who designed the other windows in the church, except the two in the vestibule. The latter (William Wilson artist 1948) are a memorial to the Reverend John A Robertson, the first minister. The architecture matches his motto: 'Only the best for St Anne's.'

286

Martello Court

87 Pennywell Gardens

Rowand Anderson, Kininmonth & Paul 1964–7

At 23 storeys (64 metres), this is the tallest residential building in Edinburgh. It was part of the Muirhouse council housing scheme, a concrete Utopia begun in 1953. When utopias fail, the architects get blamed. Muirhouse had social problems but they did not develop on drawing boards. Martello Court, like Cables Wynd (see 225), is now acknowledged as 20th-century heritage. The name refers to the Martello tower (1809) built to defend the Port of Leith during the Napoleonic Wars.

287

Granton Gas Holder No.1

ForthQuarter Park

Walter Ralph Herring architect/engineer c. 1900

Telescopic gas holder with a cylindrical steel frame in which interlocking tanks floated up from inside each other as they were filled with gas. The Edinburgh and Leith Corporation Gas Commissioners planned eight holders when the site was developed (1898–1902). One was built then; two others followed, in 1933 and 1966, since demolished.

Holder No.1 was decommissioned in 2003. The National Grid declared it 'an outdated relic, a local eyesore', but it is heritage-listed, so it survives. The city bought the site in 2018 to advance Granton Waterfront, an ambitious regeneration of post-industrial land. Granton Gasworks was so large that it had its own train station. No trains now but Gasworks Station (also by WR Herring) is still here, across from Scottish Gas (next entry).

288
Scottish Gas Headquarters
1 Waterfront Avenue
Foster + Partners, White Young Green engineers, Hyland Edgar Driver landscape design 2003

The global architects' first effort in Edinburgh, a concrete and glass box with aluminium *brise-soleil*, an atrium, open-plan offices and a call centre. Rated BREEAM Excellent, it was the first building in the architects' Granton Waterfront masterplan and set a high standard for those to follow. Also in Granton is the National Museums Collection Centre (Hoskins Architects 2015) at 242 West Granton Road, a three-storey treasure trove (more than 10 million objects), with facilities for conservation and research.

Behind Scottish Gas is Caroline Park House (1685). Its landscape was reduced and polluted by the gas works, but the house and garden are well preserved. To the west is ForthQuarter Park (2005), a biodiverse habitat for wildlife and people. Environmental clean-up was required before Foster + Partners' masterplan could implemented.

289
Madelvic House
33 Granton Park Avenue

A relic from the oldest purpose built car factory in Britain – the office of the Madelvic Motor Carriage Company, founded in 1899 by City Astronomer William Peck to exploit electric technology. The company made battery-powered vehicles driven by a fifth wheel, which inspired the logo above the door. They were tested as taxis but not a success. Madelvic, ahead of its time, went bankrupt in 1900.

290
Granton Lighthouse (Northern Lighthouse Board Depot)
22 West Harbour Road
William Burn c. 1870

The NLB was founded in 1786 to build and maintain Scotland's lighthouses

and navigational buoys. Its ships were once based in Granton Harbour. This lighthouse was built to train light keepers and to test lights; the other buildings were workshops and stores. Activity was gradually relocated and the facility closed in 2001. The NLB head office remains on George Street (see 110).

At 18–19 West Harbour Road is Powderhall Bronze, established 1989. In 2016, the foundry restored the Forsyth Globe (see 84).

291
Social Bite Village
West Shore Road

Social Bite, a startup to help feed and employ street people, opened a sandwich shop on Rose Street in 2012. In 2016, co-founder Josh Littlejohn went to Edinburgh Council and borrowed land at Granton for a temporary village for homeless folk. A prefabricated low-cost cabin, based on a prototype by Tiny House Scotland, was previewed in 2017 on St Andrew Square. The enterprise gained partners, Cyrenians and Hillcrest Housing Association, and support from companies and individuals.

The eco-friendly village, on a bracing brae overlooking the Firth of Forth, provides a safe haven and practical help to get those adrift back into society. Its ten two-bedroom units and a community hall were fabricated by Carbon Dynamic, specialists in modular manufacturing using sustainable timber. They can be moved to a new location when the lease expires.

292
Lauriston Castle
Cramond Road South

Late 16th-century tower house with 19th-century additions and Edwardian interiors. Built by the Napiers of Merchiston (see 174) on lands once held by the Forresters of Corstorphine. The tower house was extended in Jacobean style (William Burn 1827) for banker Thomas Allan, and for Lord Rutherfurd (gabled porches and landscape design, by William Playfair c. 1845). In 1902, William Reid of cabinet makers Morison & Company bought Lauriston after

selling the firm. The Reid family gifted the castle, contents and grounds overlooking the Firth of Forth to the city in 1926. There are mature monkey puzzle trees, an Italian garden, a Victorian glasshouse, croquet lawn, and a Japanese garden (opened in 2002). The property is preserved much as the Reids left it.

293
Cramond Kirk
Cramond Glebe Road

The parish, where the River Almond enters the Forth, has been a Christian site since the 6th century, dedicated to Saint Columba. The land was once a Roman fort (its footprint marked by archaeologists is in the park behind the kirk).

The kirk's tower, and a slab-roofed stone vault at the east gable, are all that remain from the medieval church, rebuilt in 1656. The tower houses a 17th-century Dutch bell, stolen for its metal value by Cromwell's troops in 1651 (an appeal to their commander, General Monck, got it back). The sanctuary has been altered periodically, radically in 1911 when the timber hammerbeam roof was fitted. There are memorials, notably a cartouche with a portrait bust of James Hope of Hopetoun (see 300), benefactor of the rebuilt church (his tomb, with an elaborate eulogy engraved, is on the outside wall). Stained glass includes three windows by Morris & Co. (Edward Burne-Jones artist) in memory of William Reid of Lauriston Castle and his brother in law.

By the gate is the counting house, where the Sunday collections were kept in a wall safe. It is said to have been restored (c. 1932) by Basil Spence. In 2014, it became the Little Gatehouse Gallery. On the south side of the kirkyard is the manse (17th century, rebuilt in 1745). Robert Walker, the minister from 1776 to 1784, was the 'Skating Minister' on Duddingston Loch (see 253).

294
Cramond Harbour

Cramond is so pretty it is hard to believe it has an industrial heritage. Eighteenth-century entrepreneurs, attracted by the water power of the

River Almond, built iron works, for which the harbour was upgraded. Cramond Iron Works was the biggest. In 1788, it was relocated to Glasgow. By 1860, only traces of Cramond's industry were left. The history of the community, from its Roman Fort to recent times, is featured in exhibits by Cramond Heritage Trust in The Maltings, one of several late 18th-century buildings on the harbour quayside. Upriver is the early 15th century Cramond Old Bridge, or 'Cramond Brig', on the old road to South Queensferry.

295
Dalmeny Kirk
Main Street, Dalmeny
12th century; enlarged 1671;
restored 1927–37
The most complete Romanesque par-ish church in Scotland. Wonderful, weathered but largely intact bestiary

on the South Doorway from a time when few folk could read; thus, pagan and biblical images dissemi-nated myths and moral lessons. Gravestones in the kirkyard also have symbols: an anchor, armorial eagle and tools of trade, for example. The kirk's guidebook explains the iconography and masons' marks inside, where arches to the vaulted chancel and apse are pat-terned with carved chevrons, and ceiling ribs spring from corbels carved with human and animal heads.

In 1671, the Rosebery Aisle was built on the north side for the Earl of Rose-bery of Dalmeny estate. There was a medieval bell tower, long gone (there is no record when). In the 1920s the minister, William Neil Sutherland, began a ten-year restoration to a plan by architect Peter Macgregor Chalmers. This included a new tower, built with stones recycled from Calton Jail, demol-ished at the time (see 77). The stones from the jail had been extracted from Dalmeny quarry, the source of the kirk's original masonry. Of interest not far from here is Kirkliston Parish Church, also Romanesque.

296

The Hawes Inn
South Queensferry

In the 11th-century, Queen Margaret established a ferry service to and from the Kingdom of Fife. The Hawes Inn, originally Newhalls Inn (1638), was a stopover for travellers waiting for or disembarking from the ferry. The 19th-century slipway is outside (the landing place was by Priory Church until 1812).

The inn is vernacular style with harled crowstepped gables facing the sea; annex by Sydney Mitchell & Wilson (1893). The ferry service ceased when the Forth Road Bridge opened in 1964. Workers building the Forth Railway Bridge (its south approach viaduct looms above) drank at the inn's bar. In 1886, Robert Louis Stevenson is said to have written part of *Kidnapped* while lodging here (South Queensferry is a key location in the novel).

297

The Forth Bridge

Benjamin Baker & John Fowler engineers, William Arrol & Co. contractor
1882–90

Three great bridges cross the Forth estuary (photo, pages 178–179) – the Forth Railway Bridge (1890), the Forth Road Bridge (1964) and Queensferry Crossing (2017). The railway bridge, which replaced the Granton train ferry, is the supreme example of Victorian engineering. It was conceived during a period of intense competition between railway companies to provide the fastest route to north-east Scotland. Two wide and windy river estuaries had to be crossed: the Forth and the Tay.

The 2.5-kilometre long, all-steel Forth Bridge was over-engineered, for good reason. The original design, a suspension bridge by Thomas Bouch, engineer for the North British Railway Company, was rejected after his Tay Bridge collapsed in a storm with fatal consequences in 1879. The unfortunate Bouch, his reputation destroyed, died shortly after and was buried in the Edinburgh's Dean Cemetery. Engineers Benjamin Baker and John Fowler, and bridge builder and engineer William Arrol, were appointed. Work was haz-

ardous. A memorial to 73 'briggers' who lost their lives during construction stands on South Queensferry's promenade; a twin is on the north shore.

'Painting the Forth Bridge' to keep it rust-free was a saying synonymous with a never-ending task. Refurbishment by Network Rail (2001–11) applied three layers of specially formulated paint good for 25 years. The bridge was designated a UNESCO World Heritage Site in 2015.

298
Priory Church of St Mary of Mount Carmel
Hopetoun Road, South Queensferry

The 15th-century Priory Church is the oldest building in South Queensferry. A monastery (or priory) was built on this site in 1440, its genesis a Carmelite friary of around 1330). After the Reformation, the property was returned to the Dundas family which had granted the grounds to the friars. Priory Church was Queensferry Parish Church until 1633, when a new one was built in the Vennel off the High Street (still there, converted in 1999 for residential use, next to the atmospheric Old Burial Ground).

Priory Church became a school, later a net loft and stables. By the 1870s, it was roofless. It was restored in 15th-century Gothic style (John Kinross architect 1890) and reconsecrated for the Scottish Episcopal Church. In the chancel are Dundas memorials; east window by Mayer of Munich (1890). Square-plan tower accessed by a medieval turnpike stair.

299
Ove Arup & Partners International
Scotstoun House, South Queensferry
Peter Foggo, Ove Arup & Partners 1966; HAA Design, Arup engineers 2010

Scottish headquarters of the international engineering practice whose expertise is seen in two of the nation's most recent iconic structures: Queensferry Crossing and the V&A Dundee.

Scotstoun House is a single-storey concrete, steel and glass classic of its time. The flat-roofed, steel-beamed, open-plan office with a clerestory-lit central space was visualised by its architect as a 'pavilion in the park' of Scotstoun House (18th-century, demolished; the gatehouse and garden walls remain).

In 2010, the Arup building was upgraded while respecting its spatial and structural integrity. Its horizontal character informed a timber-clad extension. The transition between the old and new is defined with a softly skylit void. A landscaped courtyard recalls the original walled garden. Exemplary, contextual and sustainable, rated BREEAM Excellent. The building has another distinction – Ove Arup, the pioneering 20th-century engineer, signed one of its precast concrete panels.

300
Hopetoun House
Shore Road, South Queensferry
William Bruce 1699–1710; William Adam & sons 1721–54

The old coach road along the shore west of the Forth bridges leads to a classical gateway, a wooded rise and a plateau where, like a mirage, Hopetoun House appears. It is the ancestral home of the Hope family whose origin is traced to John Hope, a 16th-century merchant with property on the Royal Mile in Edinburgh. In 1626, his grandson was appointed King's Advocate to Charles I. The wealth that later built the house was acquired by a fortunate marriage which gained ownership of lead mines in Lanarkshire.

An ornamental pond reflects the initial – and from the approach on the plateau unseen – elevation (shown here) composed in Palladian style by William Bruce, who enhanced Holyroodhouse for Charles II. At Hopetoun,

he was assisted by Alexander Edward who, according the *Dictionary of Scottish Architects*, had 'acquired much fame by his skill in architecture and drawing plans of houses and gardens'. In 1701, Edward went to France and the Low Countries on behalf of Scottish nobles, among them the Earl of Hopetoun. He visited 'the most curious and remarkable houses' and gardens, and collected and made drawings for reference. Consequently, the Hopetoun estate was transformed with a French-inspired landscape defined by formal vistas of Bruce's architecture and its hinterland.

William Adam was commissioned in 1721 to enlarge the house, which he did with a stupendous east-facing composition in Renaissance style flanked by colonnades and pavilions with baroque towers north and south. His sons John, Robert and James completed interiors fit for a king. In 1822, George IV was received by the 4th Earl and Countess of Hopetoun for lunch on the final day of his memorable visit to Edinburgh. He left by carriage, passing through the classical gateway to the coast road and Port Edgar, near South Queensferry, to sail back to London on the royal yacht.

In 1974, Hopetoun House Preservation Trust was formed to conserve and make accessible to the public the stately home, its artworks, gardens, woodland and park. The 'Scottish Versailles' remains much as it was when William Bruce first designed it and when George IV was here.

Acknowledgements

Thanks to publisher Gavin MacDougall and the team at Luath Press; to my wife Porta for her patience, editorial support and photographs, and to the architects who responded to my questions:

Aitken Turnbull Architects, Alan Dunlop, Bennetts Associates Architects, Benjamin Tindall Architects, Calum Duncan Architects, Collective Architecture, Elder & Cannon Architects, Groves-Raines Architects, Haar Architects, Hoskins Architects, James Robertson, John Kinsley Architects, Konishi Gaffney Architects, LDN Architects, Lee Boyd Architects, Malcolm Fraser, Michael Laird Architects, Oberlanders Architects, Oliver Chapman Architects, Page\Park Architects, Reiach & Hall Architects, Richard Murphy, Simpson & Brown Architects, Smith Scott Mullan Associates, Sutherland Hussey Harris Architects, 3DReid Architects.

Thanks also to Ove Arup & Partners International, Graham Construction, The Royal Incorporation of Architects in Scotland (RIAS), Royal Observatory Edinburgh Trust, and Edinburgh Libraries and Museums; and the people of Edinburgh for their unfailing courtesy when interviewed for this book.

References

An essential (and often entertaining) resource for biographies is the *Dictionary of Scottish Architects 1660–1980* **www.scottisharchitects.org.uk** For more about recent buildings see architects' websites; for architectural terms **www.lookingatbuildings.org.uk/glossary** is recommended.

City of Edinburgh Council Libraries and Museums
  www.capitalcollections.org.uk
  edinburghmuseums.org.uk
Edinburgh in 101 Objects www.edinburgh.org/101
Edinburgh World Heritage www.ewht.org.uk
Historic Environment Scotland www.historicenvironment.scot
Holyrood Palace www.rct.uk/visit/palace-of-holyroodhouse
Legacies of British Slave-ownership www.ucl.ac.uk/lbs
National Galleries of Scotland www.nationalgalleries.org
National Library of Scotland www.nls.uk
National Museum of Scotland www.nms.ac.uk
National Trust for Scotland www.nts.org.uk

Royal Incorporation of Architects in Scotland **www.rias.org.uk**

www.saltiresociety.org.uk

Scottish Parliament **www.parliament.scot/visit-and-learn**

www.urbanrealm.com

Atkins, Richard, and Emily Stephen ed. *100 Scottish Sustainable Buildings*.
Scottish Ecological Design Association 2017

Baxter, Neil and Fiona Sinclair ed. *Scotstyle: 100 Years of Scottish Architecture
1916–2015*. Edinburgh: Royal Incorporation of Architects in Scotland 2016
—Sinclair, Fiona. *Scotstyle: 150 Years of Scottish Architecture 1834–1983*.
Edinburgh: Royal Incorporation of Architects in Scotland/Scottish Academic
Press 1984

Book of the Old Edinburgh Club original series. Edinburgh: Old Edinburgh Club
1908–85

Daiches, David ed. *Edinburgh: A Travellers' Companion*. London: Constable 1986

Gifford, John, Colin MacWilliam and David Walker. *The Buildings of Scotland,
Edinburgh*. London: Penguin Books 1991

McKean, Charles. *Edinburgh: An Illustrated Architectural Guide*. Edinburgh: Royal
Incorporation of Architects in Scotland 1992

McKee, Kirsten Carter. *Calton Hill and the plans for Edinburgh's Third New Town*.
Edinburgh: Birlinn 2018

McKenzie, Ray, with Dianne King and Tracy Smith. *Public Sculpture of
Edinburgh, Volumes 1 & 2*. Liverpool: Liverpool University Press 2018

Macmillan, Duncan. *Scotland's Shrine; The Scottish National War Memorial*.
London: Lund Humphries 2014

Popiel, Alyssa Jean. *A Capital View: The Art of Edinburgh; one hundred artworks
from the City Collection*. Edinburgh: Birlinn Ltd. 2014

Stevenson, Robert Louis. *Edinburgh Picturesque Notes*. London: Seeley, Jackson
and Halliday 1879 (digital edition robert-louis-stevenson.org)

Youngson, AJ *The Making of Classical Edinburgh 1750–1840*. Edinburgh:
Edinburgh University Press 1966; reissued 2019

Walker, David M. *St Andrew's House; An Edinburgh Controversy 1912–1939*.
Edinburgh: Historic Scotland 1989

Index

Buildings, monuments, architects, artists, engineers etc. are indexed with the entry numbers (not page numbers) where they appear. Main entries are highlighted.

Luath Press Limited

committed to publishing well written books worth reading

LUATH PRESS takes its name from Robert Burns, whose little collie Luath (*Gael.*, swift or nimble) tripped up Jean Armour at a wedding and gave him the chance to speak to the woman who was to be his wife and the abiding love of his life. Burns called one of the 'Twa Dogs' Luath after Cuchullin's hunting dog in Ossian's *Fingal*. Luath Press was established in 1981 in the heart of Burns country, and is now based a few steps up the road from Burns' first lodgings on Edinburgh's Royal Mile. Luath offers you distinctive writing with a hint of unexpected pleasures.

Most bookshops in the UK, the US, Canada, Australia, New Zealand and parts of Europe, either carry our books in stock or can order them for you. To order direct from us, please send a £sterling cheque, postal order, international money order or your credit card details (number, address of cardholder and expiry date) to us at the address below. Please add post and packing as follows: UK – £1.00 per delivery address; overseas surface mail – £2.50 per delivery address; overseas airmail – £3.50 for the first book to each delivery address, plus £1.00 for each additional book by airmail to the same address. If your order is a gift, we will happily enclose your card or message at no extra charge.

Luath Press Limited
543/2 Castlehill
The Royal Mile
Edinburgh EH1 2ND
Scotland
Telephone: +44 (0)131 225 4326 (24 hours)
email: sales@luath. co.uk
Website: www. luath.co.uk